A MATTER

of

LIFE

and

DEATH

HOW TO HANDLE FAMILY AFFAIRS
DURING ILLNESS AND DEATH
AND KEEP PROBATE COURT OUT OF YOUR BUSINESS

JEHAN CRUMP-GIBSON, ESQ.

A MATTER OF LIFE AND DEATH
How to Handle Family Affairs During Illness and Death
and Keep Probate Court Out of Your Business

This book is intended solely for informational and educational purposes and does not constitute legal advice. The content provided herein is not a substitute for consultation with a licensed attorney or other qualified professional. Readers are encouraged to seek legal advice tailored to their specific circumstances from a licensed attorney in their jurisdiction.

The author and publisher of this book make no representations or warranties, expressed or implied, regarding the completeness, accuracy, or applicability of the information provided. While every effort has been made to ensure the accuracy of the content at the time of publication, laws and regulations may change, and the reader assumes full responsibility for any actions taken based on the information in this book.

The author and publisher shall not be held liable for any losses, damages, or legal consequences arising from the use or misuse of the information contained within this publication. The views expressed in this book are those of the author and do not necessarily reflect the policies or positions of any professional organization or entity.

Paperback ISBN: 979-8-218-48697-6

First Paperback Edition: December 2024
Printed in the United States of America

Edited by: Khloe's Thoughts Editing & Monique D. Mensah
Cover by: Make Your Mark Publishing Solutions
Layout by: Make Your Mark Publishing Solutions

ACKNOWLEDGMENTS

I would like to express my sincerest gratitude to my amazing clients who have entrusted me over the years with their families and their future. The inspiration for this book came from witnessing firsthand the devastating impact the probate process can have on families. I want to try to reach as many people as possible so that they don't have to experience the same distress while trying to grieve.

Monique Mensah and her amazing team at Make Your Mark Publishing Solutions deserve a standing ovation for their insightful feedback and dedication to shaping this manuscript.

Last, but certainly not least, a special thanks to my family for their unwavering support and my team at Great Lakes Legal Group PLLC. Without you all, there's simply no way I could do what I do.

This book is dedicated to my beloved grandparents in heaven: Rev. Dr. Henry Crump, Alfred Gibson and Vivian L. Gibson. I hope I am making you proud.

"If you fail to plan, you are planning to fail"

- BENJAMIN FRANKLIN

CONTENTS

INTRODUCTION

There are a lot of scary things in this world: violence in our streets, inequities, killer clowns, lashes that look like curtains, the price of meat and dairy...the list goes on. But one of the scariest things we do not talk enough about is probate court.

Probate courts are responsible for appointing guardians and conservators for individuals who can no longer manage their affairs due to physical or mental health issues. They also oversee the distribution of property a person may leave behind after death, if the property is solely in the deceased person's name with no beneficiary. The probate process often involves several court hearings, tedious filings, and can be extremely time consuming—even when all parties involved are getting along well.

If you do not take the time to *plan*, your loved ones will end up there, often forced to hire attorneys, who bill hundreds of dollars an hour, to navigate the complicated probate process. Your loved ones will be subjected to public hearings, where anyone attending can hear sensitive details about your family and finances.

Sure, no one wants to talk about their own mortality, but I want to let you in on a little secret—it is real—whether you acknowledge it or not. A client once told me, "Well, I guess we are all born on hospice." Morbid, right? Well, it's true. I told him I was going to start saying this. The reality is, no one knows when the time will come for them to depart this place or if they will ever be in a position where they cannot take care of their own affairs. Due to this, you should live life to the fullest but also plan for the unexpected. It can really save you and your loved ones a world of trouble.

There are so many myths out there about estate planning, and one of them is that you must be rich to do it. My theory? If you're not rich, you can't afford *not* to. An estate is simply any property that you own, whether this is household goods, jewelry, a bank account, a business, a car, or an insurance policy. An estate plan is a binding set of instructions that assigns the person who will handle your estate and describes what they're supposed to do with it. Your estate must go through the same process as that of some of your favorite celebrities who have millions of dollars. If that's the case, what do you think will be left over for your loved ones when you pass away if you don't plan accordingly?

In my fifteen years of practicing in probate court as a licensed attorney in Michigan, I have seen the unthinkable— families torn apart, with their dearly departed turning over in their graves because of drama over worthless junk and what amounts to nothing more than pennies in the grand scheme of things. Some folks get really ugly when a death occurs in the family, even the ones Ma Dear swore would never act up. Well, guess what, Ma Dear, she did, and you left the rest of your family behind, unequipped to deal with the foolishness.

Over the years, whenever I did estate planning seminars, had client meetings, or told cautionary tales (omitting names and specifics, of course), people would say, "You really should write a book." I usually shrugged it off, but then the lightbulb went off. *I* should *write a book!* So, I went to work, writing a collection of "scared straight" stories to get the word out about the importance of getting your affairs in order.

Probate is not as sexy as some of the other legal topics often glamourized by the entertainment industry in movies, documentaries, and television series, but it is the one area that will touch *everyone*. Why? Because *everyone* ages and may deal with health issues, and we will all ultimately die. Why not plan accordingly, so the people you've chosen can privately handle your affairs according to your wishes without court involvement?

So, here it is—a page-turner, with stories *loosely* inspired by real-life probate cases in Michigan, including a glossary with important definitions and an index of resources that can help you avoid the nightmare known as probate court to the best of your ability. These are general tips and practical advice that cover the most common scenarios that can land you in probate court.

I must give the disclaimer that this is *not* formal legal advice. Reading this book does not form an attorney-client relationship. There is also no guarantee that probate court can always be avoided. The forms at the end of this book are general templates for the everyday person and are for informational purposes only. I always recommend you consult with a licensed attorney who specializes in estate planning _where you live_ to make sure you're protected. And after you read this, you will see why that is so important (hopefully).

JEHAN CRUMP-GIBSON, ESQ.

GLOSSARY

Beneficiary	A person or entity who receives money or benefits from something, for example, a life insurance policy, bank account or even a Trust or Will. Some banks or institutions may also refer to this as a transfer-on-death (TOD) or payable-on-death (POD).
Conservatorship/ Conservator	A court-ordered arrangement that gives a person (the conservator) the authority to manage the financial affairs of someone the court has determined is unable to do so for themselves. This can be because of a physical or mental health issue, age, confinement, or disappearance.
Estate/ Estate Plan	An estate refers to the total assets a person owns (bank accounts, personal effects, life insurance policies, investments, businesses, etc.). An estate plan is simply a strategy for managing and distributing someone's estate in the event they become

	unable to do so for themselves, or when they pass away. Putting together an estate plan helps avoid probate court. All estates do not have to go through probate if planning is properly done.
Guardianship/ Guardian	A court-ordered arrangement that gives a person (the guardian) the authority to manage the personal activities or affairs of someone the court has determined unable to make or communicate informed decisions. Among other things, this can be because of a physical or mental health issue or age. This includes care and placement decisions.
Guardian Ad Litem/ GAL	In the probate context, a Guardian Ad Litem or GAL is the person appointed by the court to investigate filed petitions and make a recommendation to the Court that is in the best interests of the person the proceedings involve. For example, if someone files a petition for guardianship, the court will appoint the GAL to visit the alleged incapacitated person, explain to them their rights, investigate the suitability of the proposed guardian and other relevant matters, then report back to the Court. This person bills the alleged

	incapacitated individual or, if they do not have sufficient funds, the county that the probate court sits in.
Ladybird Deed	This is a specific type of deed that transfers property to a person or entity. As of now, Ladybird Deeds are only allowed in Michigan, Florida, Texas, West Virginia, and Vermont. Named after President Lyndon B. Johnson's wife, it allows you to maintain control over your property while you are still living. You can sell it, refinance it, rent it out, or even give it away if you want. If it is still in your name when you pass away, it will automatically pass to the person (or people), or entity you named on the deed, without the need for probate court. This is different than a Quit Claim Deed, which people will often use, not realizing it adds someone to your deed at that moment, giving them the same rights to your property as you have.
Letter of Authority	This is the legal document issued by the probate court that grants the Personal Representative (see definition) of the estate the authority to act on behalf of a deceased person's estate.

Living Trust	This is also known as a Revocable Trust or sometimes just a "Trust." It is a legal arrangement established by someone that directs distribution of assets without the need for probate court involvement. It is a Living Trust or Revocable Trust because it is set up during someone's lifetime and they can change the terms of it at any time while they are alive, as long as they have sound mind to do so. I compare a Trust to a flower vase. Your assets are the flowers (your house, your bank accounts, life insurance policies, etc.). As long as your flowers are in the vase (the Trust), they will be distributed in accordance with your wishes, without the need for probate court. In most cases, it is truly the best way to avoid probate court.
Personal Representative	Also known as Executor, the person who is appointed by the probate court to manage and distribute a deceased person's estate, meaning property that belongs only to the person who passed. In Michigan, property in someone's name alone with no living beneficiary will have to go to probate. There are no exceptions.

JEHAN CRUMP-GIBSON, ESQ.

Power of Attorney/ POA	A legal document that gives someone the authority to manage affairs on a person's behalf. There are Powers of Attorney for healthcare decisions and for finances. They can become active when you sign them or only in the event you become unable to manage your own affairs. These documents help to avoid guardianship and conservatorship proceedings in Probate Court. A person should not sign these documents if they no longer have sound mind to do so.
Probate/ Probate Court	Probate generally refers to the process through which a deceased person's property is distributed. It is necessary when someone passes away with property in their name alone, with no living beneficiary. Probate Court is the court that handles the probate process. Probate Court also handles guardianship and conservatorship matters.
Testamentary Letter	Another name for the Letter of Authority. Often, banks and other financial institutions will ask for this document before giving anyone access to accounts that were in a deceased person's name alone.

| Will | The full name is a Last Will and Testament. This is essentially an instruction sheet. It tells the court who you want to manage and distribute your property when you pass away and who you want to receive it. It does not avoid probate court like a Trust does and does not override beneficiary designations on your accounts or individuals named on a property deed. |

CHAPTER 1

A MILLION HEIRS

Well, not literally a million—more like twenty-six. Picture it: Sicily, 1938 …

Kidding. I just loved how Sophia from the 1980s sitcom *The Golden Girls* started her stories. Anyway, picture it: Uncle Bill—let's call him Unc—is seventy-six years old. He worked at one of the big autos for over thirty years until he retired at age sixty-two. A couple of years before he retired, one of his buddies from work told him he was using the free union benefit to get his affairs in order. He told Unc he should do the same.

Unc said to his buddy, "For what? I've never been married, and I have no kids. I don't have much. Why would I waste my time?"

Basking in his retirement, Unc begins spending his time fishing and bowling, never thinking about any of that stuff his buddy talked to him about again. He spends a lot of time with his favorite niece, Sally, and her family, who live about fifteen minutes away from him in Michigan. He stays in touch with Sally's sister, Theresa, who lives in Nevada.

Unc's parents passed away some time ago. He is the second to the youngest of ten children. Some of his brothers and sisters are still living; some of them passed away before him. The siblings that passed away have children who are still living, but Unc doesn't talk to any of them. He hasn't seen some of them since their parents passed; others, he hasn't seen since they were toddlers.

In his golden years, Unc's health, unfortunately, starts failing him. He has diabetes that has gone unmanaged for years, which has impacted his kidneys. In the last year, he has been receiving dialysis three times a week. He does not get around like he used to and needs someone to come in from time to time to help him. Sally comes by to check on Unc as much as possible, but she has two small children and owns a restaurant with her husband. She talks to Unc about hiring caregivers to come in to help three days a week or so. He agrees to let her hire them.

In addition to his physical health issues, Unc has also been suffering from dementia for quite some time. Most days, he still recognizes Sally, but some days, he calls her Martha (Sally's mom, who passed twenty years ago). He is extremely forgetful, does not really understand what assets he has, and simply cannot manage his financial matters anymore.

Sally has been writing out checks for his bills and having

him sign them (yes, checkbooks still exist). Unc still receives hard copies of his bank statements in the mail, and Sally can see the funds are dwindling due to the regular household bills and the caregivers. His monthly pension payment and social security check only go so far. She starts kicking in out of her own pocket but realizes she cannot do this for long because pulling from her household finances is causing strife with her husband.

She goes to Unc's credit union to get access to his IRA's so she can keep things going. She wants to keep Unc in his home where he is comfortable. He is doing well with the at-home care. He certainly has the money to pay for it—she just needs access.

Sally enters the credit union branch and signs in to see someone. She walks back to the banker's partitioned cube, sits down, and explains what is going on.

Tom, the banker, asks Sally if she has power of attorney over Unc. She is shocked by the question. Honestly, she doesn't really know what that is. She responds, "I don't think so. I'm his only family here, and I arrange for his care and take care of all his bills." She pulls out bank statements and canceled checks from her tote bag. "See? I handle everything for him already."

Tom replies, "I understand, but I cannot give you access to your uncle's accounts or provide you with any information about them. You either have to come back with a power of attorney or letters of conservatorship from a probate court."

Sally balks. "Probate court? I don't want to go there!"

Sally gathers her things and hurries out of the bank. Rob, one of her favorite customers at her restaurant, is well connected. She thinks, *I'll talk to him when he comes in for breakfast tomorrow!*

Thankfully, Rob knows exactly who she should call. He gives her the contact information for a lawyer to help her with the power of attorney over Unc.

Sally contacts the lawyer to have a power of attorney drafted. The lawyer asks her several questions about Unc's physical and mental state. She describes in detail his diagnoses and his behaviors. The lawyer explains to her that he doesn't believe Unc has the legal capacity to sign a power of attorney, which is a document that allows an individual to designate a person to manage their affairs if they become unable. A healthcare power of attorney helps to avoid guardianship proceedings in probate court, while a financial power of attorney helps avoid conservatorship proceedings.

I understand, but I cannot give you access to your uncle's accounts or provide you with any information about them. You either have to come back with a power of attorney or letters of conservatorship from a probate court.

Sally says, "Well, can't I just sign something? He's okay with me handling his finances."

The attorney tells her, "It's too late. You wouldn't want to get in trouble for having him sign something he didn't have the sound mind to sign. We don't have a choice. We now have to file a petition for conservatorship so a court can appoint you to handle your uncle's finances. You might as well go ahead and petition the court to get guardianship, so you can manage his care. You will eventually run into a problem with healthcare providers too."

Sally's head is spinning. She has no idea where to start, so she has no choice but to pay to retain the lawyer.

This opens up a potential can of worms in the court proceedings. Why? Unc's siblings have an interest in the proceedings now. Since he is not married, his parents are deceased, and he has no kids, his siblings are first in line for consideration to handle his affairs. Sally's lawyer must provide these siblings with the petitions and a notice of the court date, and any of them can object to Sally serving as guardian or conservator—despite the fact that they do not have much to do with him.

Sally is fit to be *tied*. She pleads with the attorney, "I'm the only one who has been taking care of him!"

She manages to be appointed by the court as Unc's guardian and conservator after a few hearings, allowing her to manage Unc's healthcare decisions and his finances.

Then, the unexpected happens—Unc passes away one month after Sally is appointed. Now, since all his property was solely in his name, it is in probate, and the "million heirs" start circling like buzzards on roadkill.

Sally has to pay another retainer to the lawyer to open a decedent's estate, which is a proceeding in probate court that will ultimately distribute the property Unc owned. Unc's living siblings and the children of his deceased siblings will now *all* inherit a piece of the pie. This means twenty-two relatives are standing in line to inherit something from Unc's estate, even though he hadn't spoken to nearly all of them in years.

Sally and the lawyer start receiving phone calls from the relatives. They've turned into investigative internet professionals, searching for the value of Unc's house online, seeing how much a sale would yield. One day, one of the nieces calls and asks how long this process will take because she wants her teeth done.

Sally is furious about this. She calls the lawyer handling the case. Sobbing, she exclaims, "How is this fair? These people don't even know my uncle! They are only related to him by blood. They have no relationship with him. They didn't even come to the funeral! Can't you do something about this?"

The lawyer tells her, "Sally, it may not be fair, but it is the law. What's morally wrong is not legally wrong."

While the estate is open, one of Unc's other siblings, who has four children, passes. Now, *those* four children will stand in their parents' place and inherit.

In the end, Unc's estate ends up being divided amongst twenty-six heirs, most of whom had never talked to or met Unc.

You're probably fit to be *tied*, as the old folks say, right? You should be. This happens more often than I care to admit.

HOW TO AVOID THIS

If Unc would've had his estate plan done when his work buddy recommended it, he would have had powers of attorney prepared in the event he became unable to manage his affairs. This would have avoided the conservatorship and guardianship proceedings, and Sally would have been able to access the retirement accounts to pay for the caregivers and other expenses (see Appendix I, Appendix IV).

Since he only had a relationship with two of his nieces and only wanted to provide for them, Unc could have had a trust drafted and moved those assets to the trust for their benefit (Appendix II). This would have included his house and various bank accounts.

Even if Unc did not set up a trust, he could have named his beloved nieces as beneficiaries or added a transfer-on-death designation to his bank accounts. This would have allowed the money in the accounts to go straight to his nieces without the need for probate court. Unc also could have signed a ladybird deed for his house, since he lived in one of the five states that currently allows them. A ladybird deed allows an individual to maintain control over their house while they're still living. The home can be sold, refinanced, rented out or even given away if the person so chooses. If it is still in the individual's name when they pass away, it will automatically pass to the person (or people) listed on the deed, without the need for probate court.

This strategy would have helped Sally avoid probate court, and twenty-four out of twenty-six relatives, with whom Unc did not have a relationship, would not have benefited upon his death.

CHAPTER 2

CAIN AND ABEL(LA)

Tim is fifty-eight years old and healthy by all accounts. For years, he's worked in managerial positions for large corporations. He was married for twenty years, but the marriage ended in divorce, and he has one child, a twenty-four-year-old daughter, Sue, who is the apple of his eye.

After Sue graduates from college, she moves in with Tim to save a little money and get on her feet. They live in Tim's large suburban home together, with Sue having her own apartment of sorts in the basement, as it includes its own bathroom, bedroom, and mini-kitchen.

Tim meets Yvette and ultimately falls in love. His plan is to eventually marry her. Although Tim is not sick, he often shares with Yvette his wishes if something ever happens to him. He mentions to her that he has a life insurance policy and a few investment accounts. He also tells her that after his divorce, he named his sister Julie as beneficiary on the life insurance policy, which has a $500,000 death benefit— meaning, if he passes, Julie will receive a $500,000 check.

He did this because Sue is young, so he trusts Julie to manage the money for her. He doesn't want Sue to get a $500,000 check at a young age, with no real financial experience. Julie is the sister he has always been closest to, and he trusts she will do what's best for Sue if something ever happens to him.

Tim also knows Sue and Julie had a close relationship while Sue was growing up. Julie was her favorite aunt. But Sue knows nothing about the insurance policy or much about her dad's assets at all. She certainly never asks because, in her mind, Dad is always there and will always be there.

Tim has a thing for hot rides. He has driven one for years and wants a new one. One day, he drives to the dealership and puts a $2,500 deposit on a special-order Chevy Camaro. This is going to be his best one yet. He runs a few more errands in the area then gets on the highway to head home. While driving, Tim begins to feel tightness in his chest and has trouble breathing.

Cars behind him notice that he begins slowing down. A police officer happens to be inside one of those cars. Tim manages to pull the car over to the shoulder, and the police officer determines he is having a medical episode. The officer calls for an ambulance, and Tim is transported to the nearest hospital, where he, heartbreakingly, dies shortly after he arrives.

Needless to say, Sue is devastated and confused. She begins the process of trying to handle her father's final arrangements. With her mom and her dad's sisters by her side, she is able to get through the funeral and burial.

The evening of the funeral and repast, the family goes back to Tim's house. Family and friends are in and out, eating from the spread of catfish, chicken wings, spaghetti, greens, and more. As Sue finally gains an appetite, she makes herself a plate then goes into the kitchen.

Sue's aunts start inquiring about money. Julie asks, "What are you planning on doing with the house? Can you manage all that by yourself? What else did your dad have? How much money was in the bank?"

Sue is taken aback by the intrusive questioning mere hours after they've laid her dear father to rest. She mutters, "I...I don't know" and runs downstairs with tears in her eyes.

Julie goes down to Sue's room. "Baby, we didn't mean to upset you," she says. "You know your dad and I were so close. I just want to make sure you're good, that's all." They hug and Sue heads off to bed in her room at Tim's house.

It takes Sue a few weeks to muster up the strength, but she realizes her dad's affairs aren't going to handle themselves. She knows his mortgage must be paid, and she certainly can't pay it herself. She begins by contacting her dad's job. They connect her with the institution that holds his retirement account as well as the insurer for his life insurance policy. She then contacts her dad's CPA, who is a family friend. She has the death certificate and provides it to the various financial institutions.

Unfortunately, the house is in her dad's name alone as well as his bank accounts. The mortgage company and the bank tell her she needs testamentary letters in order to access the information. She is baffled. Her next call is to her mother, who calls the lawyer that handled her and Tim's divorce. The divorce lawyer connects Sue with another lawyer who practices probate law. The probate lawyer tells Sue that in order to get a testamentary letter, which gives her authority to access Tim's assets, she has to open up an estate in probate court and be appointed personal representative—the person who handles all the final affairs for the estate, like payment of debts, taxes, and distribution of the property to whomever is entitled to receive it. In the absence of a will or trust, those entitled people are determined by state law, whether they're the preferred recipient of the assets or not.

Frustrated and overwhelmed, Sue knows she has no choice and retains the attorney, which costs her a few thousand dollars just to start. As they are going through a list of assets, the attorney tells her that any assets for which she was listed as beneficiary, she does not have to go through the probate process. The insurance company will simply cut a check to the beneficiary, which Sue assumes is her. They file the documents to open the estate in probate court.

Sue faxes in her dad's death certificate to start the process to receive the life insurance proceeds. She also faxes in estate paperwork just in case. The insurance company takes about two weeks to get back to her, which she thinks is strange. Much to her shock, she is notified that the proceeds from the policy have been paid already. The representative tells her that someone by the name of Julie Doe has already faxed a death certificate and completed beneficiary paperwork. They sent the check for the full amount of the policy to her the previous week.

Sue is outdone! She calls her aunt Julie immediately but is sent to voicemail. She calls her back three more times and sends two texts, with no response. Reeling from the shock, Sue calls her dad's girlfriend, Yvette, and her mom. Yvette is shocked to hear Julie is ignoring Sue's calls. She shares with Sue the conversation Tim had with her about his intentions

In the absence of a will or trust, those entitled people are determined by state law, whether they're the preferred recipient of the assets or not.

before he passed. She suggests that Sue send Julie an email, since she can't get through to her by phone.

Sue sends Aunt Julie a long email, explaining that she knows her dad's intentions for the funds and urges her to do the right thing and turn the money over. She then calls the probate attorney, crying. She wants to see what options there are. The attorney explains that there are very few scenarios in which someone can legally contest a life insurance beneficiary designation. He tells her that unless there is some sort of fraud or proof that Tim did not have the mental capacity to change his beneficiary, there is nothing to be done.

The attorney sends a subpoena to the insurance company to obtain all the records concerning the policy. They get the records back and confirm that Tim did, in fact, change the beneficiary to Julie after his divorce, validating the conversation Yvette previously shared.

Tim trusted Julie to do the right thing, but she did not. There is nothing the law can do for Sue. To date, Sue still has not heard from her aunt. She will never see that $500,000 her dad intended for her.

I know what you're thinking, the same thing anyone would think—Julie is president of the Scumbag Club. She is someone you want five minutes with outside. How could she possibly do this to her brother's only child? She knew he'd trusted her to handle things for Sue's benefit. How callous! But unfortunately, these things happen all the time. Humans are imperfect, and some are more flawed than others. This is why you should not leave anything to chance. After all, you'll be gone and won't be able to do anything about it.

HOW TO AVOID THIS

If Tim did not want the life insurance proceeds or any other property to go straight into his young daughter's hands, he could have set up a living trust (Appendix II- for unmarried individuals or III for married couples) and then named that trust as the beneficiary on the policy. That way, when he passed away, the proceeds would've gone straight into the trust.

Your property is like a flower, and a living trust is like a flower vase. The trust holds the property and keeps it from going to probate. Your house, bank accounts, insurance policies and your business interests are all flowers. As long as you place them in the flower vase (the living trust), they will go to whomever you want in the way you want when you pass away, without the need for court involvement.

The trust terms would have stated at what age Sue could get the money and any other conditions Tim wanted to put in place. He could've still provided for her in the way he wanted to, even though he was gone.

Whomever he would've named as trustee, which really means administrator, would be required to follow the trust terms in distributing the assets to Sue. The money would've been saved and eventually disbursed for

Sue's benefit. The check for the life insurance proceeds would not have been issued directly to Julie. But since the proceeds were paid to Julie, she was under no legal obligation to give the money to Sue or provide for her. Had the trust been the beneficiary instead of Julie, she would have been forced to "do the right thing."

CHAPTER 3

BIG MAMA DRAMA

D oris "Big Mama" Jones is ninety-three years old. Her husband passed away about fifteen years ago. She does not have much, but she owns the home she lives in free and clear and receives a social security check. She is essentially bed ridden and weak but still able to communicate. She can recall things from her young adult years, like when her children were young, but her short-term memory is terrible. For the most part, she still recognizes most of her family members, especially her beloved daughters.

She has four daughters and several grandchildren and nieces. Tension has been brewing for years with the daughters. Betty, the oldest, is with Big Mama every day. After her husband passed, she left Indiana, where her adult children and grandchildren stay, to live with Big Mama full time in Michigan. She transports Big Mama to doctor appointments and either directly provides her care at home or makes sure one of her nieces is there to step in if she is unable—and that is rare.

Theresa, the second youngest sister, is "that one," high off the hog. She went off to school, got a degree, and is a supervisor at that good *government* job. She turns her nose up at the rest of the siblings, who did not seek higher education. Betty and Theresa are like oil and water, always bickering like Teri and Maxine from the 1990s classic movie *Soul Food*. Theresa constantly complains about Betty and critiques her handling of their mother's care but hardly ever makes any efforts to relieve her. She's the one who pays the bills.

There are some hiccups ever so often, but everything is relatively smooth sailing until one day, when Betty and Theresa get into a heated argument because Theresa announced there is money coming in from a lawsuit that was filed on Big Mama's behalf when she fell while unsupervised in a rehab facility. Betty feels as though Theresa is making plans for Big Mama's money without discussing it with the entire family. The argument gets so bad that Theresa calls Betty a "miserable old &$*%$," and Betty slaps her—hard! An open-palm, might-as-well-have-gotten-th

This means a third party is paid to handle Big Mama's finances— pay her bills, coordinate benefits, etc. This person will also make care and placement decisions. Big Mama's major life decisions are now in the hands of a stranger.

e-powder-first slap. The gloves are off at this point, literally and figuratively.

After the brawl breaks up, Theresa hires a lawyer and files for guardianship so she, alone, can make Big Mama's healthcare decisions. She also files for conservatorship, so she can handle the money. Betty hires her own lawyer, refusing to let Theresa win. She also wants to be appointed over Big Mama's affairs.

Before the court date, Theresa starts restricting who can come to the house. She even threatens to evict their younger sister Stacey and her daughter, who are staying there temporarily, if they do not get their own place.

Betty's lawyer schedules a meeting to discuss case strategy and expectations. She asks Betty if her younger sisters, Tina and Stacey, are on her side or Theresa's. Betty explains that neither can be trusted to stand for what is right. Tina relies on Theresa to help her financially with her children, so she will not dare go against her, even if she does think Theresa is wrong. Stacey loathes Tina because *gasp* there was some hanky panky between Tina and Stacey's husband years prior. Stacey doesn't think her other sisters stood up for her when it happened, so she's mad at all of them. Of course, when these ladies get to court, it is going to be a battle.

While this knock-down-drag-out fight is ensuing, decisions need to be made for Big Mama until the court decides who will manage her affairs. It takes three minutes into the first hearing for the judge to see that these sisters can barely agree on the color of the sky, so he appoints a third party to oversee Big Mama's affairs until the conclusion of the case, which is quite common in probate court. This means a third party is *paid* to handle Big Mama's finances—pay her bills, coordinate benefits, etc. This person will also make care and placement decisions. Big Mama's major life decisions are now in the hands of a stranger.

The judge also appoints a guardian ad litem (GAL) to investigate the petitions that were filed before the court— someone else who gets paid when proceedings are filed. When the court-appointed GAL goes out to visit Big Mama, Betty lets her in and takes her to the room where Big Mama's hospital bed is set up. The GAL introduces herself to Big Mama and chats with her for a bit. Big Mama talks about the weather, church, and quite a few other things.

The GAL then asks her, "Ma'am, who do you want to handle your affairs?"

The room falls quiet. Big Mama either doesn't want to decide or doesn't understand what the GAL is asking her. She sits quietly with her eyes down. The only thing she tells the GAL is, "I love all my girls just the same."

It becomes clear to the GAL that Big Mama knows her girls are fighting, whether she says something or not. The GAL then talks to each of the daughters separately. By the time she finishes, she feels like she needs a massage and several adult beverages. She writes her report to submit to the court. Her recommendation is that a third party continues to handle Big Mama's affairs due to the discord amongst the daughters.

Months go by, with countless hearings, endless hours, and thousands of dollars in attorney's fees, before the case finally settles at mediation, which the judge has ordered. The only way for the family to keep a third party out of Big Mama's affairs is to come together but not before relationships are fractured even further. What should be Big Mama's glory years before she goes on home are filled with strife amongst her children, whom she knows she raised better than this.

HOW TO AVOID THIS

Had Big Mama signed powers of attorney long before her decline, it would have been clear who she thought was in the best position to handle her affairs. Now that Big Mama is in a poor mental state, it is too late to execute power of attorney, as you are required to have sound mind to do so. This could have gone a long way in avoiding probate court proceedings, specifically conservatorship for her finances and guardianship for her care and placement decisions.

In the absence of powers of attorney, a court hearing requires evidence from interested parties for who should be the one to manage someone's affairs. This seems like a simple concept, but it's not. I've seen guardianship and conservatorship disputes last well over a year, wasting money, time, and resources that could've been directed elsewhere, namely to the person for whom decisions needed to be made.

CHAPTER 4

OIL AND WATER

Carl Phillips is divorced, with two adult children in their forties. After retiring as a journeyman, he bought a boat, a motorcycle, and lives comfortably in his double-wide home.

His two daughters, Claire and Shelly, have been like oil and water since childhood. This is no petty siblings' quarreling: with siblings like them, who needs enemies?

How bad is it? When they were teenagers, Claire called the police on Shelly simply because she made her mad. Shelly had marijuana on her and was arrested. They never recovered from this and remain at odds.

Over the years, Carl has supported Claire through drug habits, criminal troubles, excessive debt—the whole nine. However, Carl does not agree with Shelly's lifestyle, so they do not speak much at all. This obviously creates more resentment in Shelly and has caused her to avoid Claire and her dad for quite some time. Shelly moves from Michigan to Arizona to get away from it all.

Carl is known to "party," even though he is well into his sixties. He makes a habit of spending time at the local strip clubs, drinking heavily, and dabbling in recreational drugs frequently. His lifestyle eventually catches up to him. Just after his sixty-seventh birthday, his health begins declining. He begins losing weight without trying. His appetite is poor, his abdomen is swollen, and he is nauseous and vomiting. Being a macho man who loathes doctors, he has no plans to go in for an examination. In fact, he hasn't been to a doctor's office in nearly ten years. He figures it's a bug that will pass.

A month goes by, and it becomes clear to Claire that he isn't getting better. Carl finally relents and allows Claire to take him in. He is diagnosed with advanced cirrhosis of the liver. After the diagnosis, Carl must go to lots of doctor's appointments, and Claire normally drives him.

Soon, it is determined that Carl will need a liver transplant. In the meantime, Claire often goes back and forth from Michigan to Texas, where her boyfriend lives. When she leaves, Carl *still* hangs out with younger women who love to party and do drugs, despite how sick he is, believing that if he's on his way out, he might as well live life to the fullest. YOLO!

Carl never bothers to do any estate planning, because, firstly, he doesn't really think he's going anywhere anytime soon. Secondly, he assumes his two daughters will naturally inherit his stuff if something does happen to him. He's right about the latter, since he's not married, but what he doesn't realize is that his children will not get his assets without having to go to probate court. And the last thing "Oil and Water" need is to end up in court with something else to battle about.

Unfortunately, they will find out, sooner than later, how bad that battle will be, as Carl passes away eight months after his diagnosis. When he passes away, his daughters realize his home, retirement accounts, and life insurance policy are in his name alone, and he has not named beneficiaries. He also had a motorcycle, a boat, several classic cars, and personal effects that he'd collected over the years, including quite a few collectors' items like valuable antiques and coins.

Naturally, Claire believes she is entitled to her pick of the litter because she was the one traveling back and forth, attempting to manage Carl's care. Claire takes her dad's wallet and uses a few of his credit cards to cover her personal affairs and pay for some of the funeral expenses.

When Shelly gets to town, she and Claire are getting along for the first time since 1979. But things go off the rails when Shelly tries to enter their dad's house with her old key—she can't get in the front door. Remembering a trick to enter through the side door without unlocking it, she finally gets inside the house and is blown away. There are drugs and beer bottles all over the place, and it looks like their dad's room has been ransacked. Shelly notices that his wallet is nowhere to be found and a few items of value are missing. She confronts Claire, who denies taking them.

Shelly gets a call the next day from a friend who is dating the owner of a pawn shop close to Carl's house. She finds out that Claire is trying to hock the items Shelly *knows* she took. Shelly calls a lawyer, sparking the beginning of a three-and-a-half-year battle in probate court.

A judge appoints a third party over the estate because good ol' Oil and Water can

He's right about the latter, since he's not married, but what he doesn't realize is that his children will not get his assets without having to go to probate court.

barely be in the room together. This third party, a representative from a local law firm, is a total stranger to them. From criminal accusations to fighting over frivolous items in a storage unit, this is a Tyson-Holyfield match up. In the end, the lawyers collectively made $100,000 in legal fees.

HOW TO AVOID THIS

Carl had several options, but he needed a trust. He could not have left assets, like his home and vehicles, to both of his children to share equal ownership because it would've undoubtedly caused a war. Think about it, if he'd simply added them both to the deed for the house, it would have forced them to be joint owners and they'd have to agree on sharing expenses and what to do with the property. Given Claire's financial issues, adding her to the deed would have also exposed the house to Claire's creditors and liabilities. Since Carl owned the home and multiple other assets, and had warring children out for blood, he could have set up a trust, put all his assets in the trust, and designated a third party to distribute the assets without the need for probate court.

CHAPTER 5

GRANDMA'S BABIES; AUNTIE'S MAYBE

Deborah Jones has two daughters. She worked as a schoolteacher and retired after thirty years of service. Her husband passed away at sixty-nine years old. Deborah remains in the house they purchased together. She lives a simple life and does not have many bills. The house and the car are paid off, and for income, she receives a small survivor's pension from her husband, another small pension from her job, and social security.

Both of her daughters have children. Her daughter Melissa lives in Kansas. Her daughter Samantha lives about fifteen minutes from Deborah, in Michigan. One year, Samantha suddenly and tragically passes away from a heart attack. After her passing, Samantha's children distance themselves from their grandmother and aunt, choosing to move to different states and keep to themselves.

Deborah's health begins failing after complications from untreated diabetes. She has to go to a facility because she cannot be home alone. This does not sit well with Melissa, who packs up her things, sells her house, and moves back to Michigan to take care of her mom. She moves into the house with Deborah. She uses her own money to make upgrades to the bathroom and bedroom to make them more accessible for Deborah, who can only walk with a walker.

One day, Deborah sits Melissa down and tells her about her final wishes. It is not a conversation Melissa wants to have, but Deborah is insistent. Deborah tells Melissa she had a will done not long after her husband passed; however, this was about fifteen years ago. She tells Melissa to go look in her Bible that she keeps on the dresser. In it is Deborah's Last Will and Testament folded in an envelope. Melissa reads over the Will and sees that Deborah left all her assets to her children. Satisfied that everything will be in order when Deborah passes, Melissa files the Will with the court for safekeeping and keeps a photocopy at the house. Melissa continues to care for her mother until she passes away seven years later at ninety-one years old.

At the funeral, Melissa sees her sister's children, Michael and Tammy, for the first time in a decade. The interaction is quite tense. Melissa harbors resentment because Michael and

Tammy rarely checked on their grandmother when she was alive. Michael and Tammy harbor resentment because they feel like the family abandoned them after their mom passed away. At the repast, other family members overhear Michael and Tammy badmouthing their aunt Melissa and saying they will "make her pay." Melissa is shocked, hurt, and confused. She has no clue what they mean by that. After all, she is due to inherit the house and any other assets Deborah had. It is written clearly in the Will.

Both Deborah and Melissa assumed that the house, which is the major asset, would automatically go to Melissa. Well, what they didn't realize is that the Will, in and of itself, will not help Melissa avoid probate court. They also didn't realize how the language in the Will was written. Once Samantha passed away, her interests went to her children. So, this means that once Deborah passed, half the interest of the house would go to Melissa and the other half to Samantha's children.

Melissa finds out the hard way that the Will doesn't serve the purpose she thought it would. She ultimately has to call a lawyer to get assistance with opening a decedent's estate in probate court to distribute Deborah's property . Since her niece and nephew are heirs, they must be served with the paperwork. Melissa thinks, *Well, I live here. This has been my home,*

> *Well, what they didn't realize is that the Will, in and of itself, will not help Melissa avoid probate court.*

and I've put my own money into this. Why do my niece and nephew have to be involved at all? They haven't even been around.

The lawyer explains that the law is the law. If Melissa wants the house, she has to buy her niece and nephew out. Melissa is furious. She offers Michael and Tammy a nominal amount of money, far below what the home is worth. Her nephew calls an attorney and retains him. They are out for blood, making good on that promise from the repast. They file a petition with the court, requesting that Melissa be charged for rent and claiming that she is hiding assets because, from what they remember, "Granny had more than what she's saying."

The family fights for months and finally settles right before trial. Thousands of dollars are spent in lawyers' fees, which significantly reduces the amount of money they all walk away with. Melissa's niece and nephew are, now, even more estranged than they were before. They do not speak to each other at all, except through lawyers, which is such a travesty. They no longer have their mother, their father, or their grandmother, and any chance of a relationship with the last remaining relative on their mother's side has been destroyed.

HOW TO AVOID THIS

The simple Will by itself won't cut it in most cases anymore. First, it does not help you avoid probate court. Secondly, many people do not understand the issues that arise if named beneficiaries pass away and there are no explicit instructions. Deborah certainly did not anticipate that one of her children would predecease her, but she also had no idea about the fight that would ensue between her surviving daughter and grandchildren. A trust would have been perfect for Deborah. She could have placed the home in the trust and provided explicit instructions for what would happen to the house if someone unexpectedly passed away. This could happen *without* the need for probate.

CHAPTER 6

IT'S MINE BECAUSE
I SAY IT IS

B en is eighty-one years old and the youngest of twelve children. He has always taken care of his older siblings as they age. Ben lives in Tennessee. Two of his sisters, Sarah and Elsie, live together in Sarah's house in Michigan, which Sarah previously shared with her late husband for thirty years prior to his death.

Elsie has been suffering from diabetes for years, and Sarah suffers from dementia. Ben pays the second mortgage that was taken out on the home, the taxes, and insurance, and he also assists in paying for in-home caregivers.

Sarah passes away first and Elsie two years later. Neither of them has children. Ben is exhausted after burying his sisters and does not put much energy into looking into their final affairs. But he knows they did not have much money, since he was paying the lion's share of the bills anyway, so he also pays for their burials.

Five years after Elsie passed away, Ben wants to pull some equity out of his late sisters' home to make some repairs and upgrades. Ultimately, he wants to sell the property or rent it out. He thinks to himself, *I might as well make some money after all I've invested in that house.*

He contacts a lender to get started with the process. Ben fills out the application and starts providing documents. When it is time to close on the transaction, the title company sends out a report showing who the owners of the property are. It does not even dawn on Ben that he does not "technically" own the property, but he does not think it matters. It does, though, because you can't pull equity out of something that is not yours, no matter how much money you've dumped into it.

Ben then says, "No biggie … Sarah owned the house. I can send you Sarah's death certificate, and we should be fine, right?"

Wrong! The title company tells Ben he has to go to probate court to get the title to the house transferred into his name. Ben is outdone.

He gets a recommendation for a lawyer from one of the neighbors on the street because he has no idea where to start. He goes to meet with the lawyer, who asks him a series of questions, namely, who Sarah's heirs are. Since Sarah had no living parents, no children or spouse, her siblings were to inherit her property. For the siblings who predeceased her, their children will stand in their parent's shoes. Ben tells the lawyer that, besides a few estranged nieces and nephews, he is the only one left. The lawyer explains that if he cannot get ahold of those nieces and nephews, he will need to take extra steps. He cannot just act like those relatives do not exist. Ben tells the lawyer there's no way for him to know where his distant relatives are.

Ben's lawyer drafts the paperwork and files it with the court. The lawyer then takes the steps to publish notice of the proceedings in the local legal newspaper, which is a requirement in probate court when certain relatives are difficult to locate. It is simply a public announcement with details

The title company tells Ben he has to go to probate court to get the title to the house transferred into his name. Ben is outdone.

of the hearing and case. The court date comes, and the judge asks more questions about the nieces and nephews that Ben says he cannot track down.

Now, this judge is not the one to play games with. She smells the hump of dog poo before the case is even called and reads Ben and the lawyer for utter and total filth. She tells Ben that she refuses to believe he cannot track down *one* of these relatives. With social media and all the other resources on the internet, he should be able to find at least a couple of them. The lawyer begs the judge to give them two weeks to find more of the relatives instead of dismissing the case.

As Ben, his wife, and the lawyer are walking to their cars, the lawyer asks, "Is there a cousin, anyone you can think of, who can give us the whereabouts of some of these folks?"

Ben looks the lawyer squarely in the face and says, "Well yes, I can have my son call his cousins. I can also ask my brother."

The lawyer looks around for a spatula to scrape his bottom jaw up off the ground. It is clear that Ben lied about being the only one left. "I'm sorry, sir," he says, "you told me before we filed the paperwork that you were the only one left."

The two of them have a Wild West stare down. Ben simply says, "I must have been confused. I just want to get this house in my name after everything I have put into it."

The lawyer shakes his head and embarks on a mission to save this case and his reputation with the judge. After diligent efforts, they successfully track down additional relatives and serve them with the court documents. Ben must have been on Santa's nice list because they managed to get the property deeded to him and close the estate out just in time for Christmas. Thankfully, his relatives did not contest.

HOW TO AVOID THIS

In Michigan and four other states, Sarah could have drafted a Ladybird deed after her husband passed away. A Ladybird Deed would've allowed her to maintain control over the house while she was still living. She could've sold it, refinanced it, rented it out, or even given it away if she wanted. If it was still in her name when she passed away, it would've automatically passed to the person (or people) listed on the deed without the need for probate court.

Had she named Ben on the deed, he would not have had to go to probate before getting the deed in his name. All he would have had to do was file her death certificate with the county's deeds office and go about his business.

Alternatively, if Sarah had other assets, that would have justified a trust, she could have set one up and transferred the house to the trust. This would have also kept Ben out of probate court.

CHAPTER 7

GET SOMEBODY
ELSE TO DO IT

B ill has four kids. He prides himself on maintaining a close relationship with all his children. His youngest child has a different mother than his three older children.

He does not think much about estate planning; after all, he is only fifty-five. He has a home, money market account, savings account, checking accounts, a $100,000 life insurance policy, and a 401k with his job. His deceased wife is still named as the beneficiary on his 401k. No one is named on the house or the other accounts. He names his youngest child, Tracy, as beneficiary on the life insurance because he admires her "take charge" attitude and figures she will handle business if anything ever happens to him. He also trusts that Tracy will take care of final arrangements and be fair with her siblings by splitting the life insurance proceeds.

Tracy is hot and cold with her half-siblings. She has always felt like an outsider, especially because it was no secret that her father had maintained a long-term relationship with her mom while he was still married to his deceased wife, her half-siblings' mother.

Tracy is presented with an investment opportunity that excites her. She goes to Bill to ask him to borrow $10,000 for the down payment. Bill is apprehensive. Tracy always has something going on, and it never goes far. Over the years, he has let her "borrow" thousands of dollars. In his mind, he is overcompensating for his indiscretions. This time, though, he puts his foot down. He knows he has been enabling Tracy, and she will never get serious about anything if she always has Daddy's checkbook to fall back on.

Tracy is furious. She leaves her dad's house that day and vows to never speak to him again. Months go by, and Bill has not heard from Tracy but figures she will eventually cool off and reach out.

Bill is healthy by all accounts. He loves to travel and fish. Some of his favorite times are spent on the lake with his son, Kevin. One day, Bill is at the lake, fishing with Kevin. They don't catch much, but Bill is happy to spend the time with his son. As they get ready to leave, Bill gives Kevin a big hug and tells him he will see him the next day for his granddaughter, Kimberly's dance recital.

Kimberly's recital comes and goes, and Bill does not show.

This is odd. Bill never misses a recital. Kevin calls Bill's house and cell phone but gets no answer. Kevin leaves little Kimberly with her mother and drives over to Bill's. He pulls in the driveway, sees that Bill's car is there, and lets himself in through the back door. The TV is blasting in the family room. Kevin calls out to Bill and gets no answer. He walks into the living room and sees why—Bill is slumped over in the chair.

Kevin calls 9-1-1, but it's too late. Bill is gone. He had a heart attack. His body is transported to the same funeral home that handled his wife's services.

Kevin, his brother, Steve, and sister, Julia, gather at the house, shocked and devastated. They start searching the house for any

Kevin and the remaining children are left scrambling to pay for the funeral. The first place they went for resources was GoFundMe.com

paperwork that will provide a clue about what Bill's final wishes were and what accounts he has. They find an insurance policy.

Kevin calls in and tells the representative that his dad passed away. Since neither Kevin nor his siblings have the cash, they need the insurance policy to pay for the burial. The representative tells Kevin that he cannot provide any additional information about the policy and the named beneficiary will need to call in.

Kevin hangs up in frustration. They take a closer look at the paperwork and see that Tracy is the beneficiary. Steve looks at Kevin, and Kevin looks at Julia with an expression that says "This is all you." Julia calls Tracy to notify her that their dad passed away and asks her to come over.

Tracy takes her sugar sweet time and shows up two hours later. Her half-siblings tell her they need to give the funeral home the information for the insurance policy and she has to call in because she's the beneficiary. They should have known after they saw the twinkle in her eye how this story would end.

Tracy says, "Okay, I'll call them tomorrow."

She does call but asks them to process the check and send it directly to her. She then meets her half-siblings at the funeral home to finalize the arrangements. She takes a look around and says she does not want to use that funeral home.

In shock, Kevin says, "Trace, Dad is here, and we need to move forward with burying him."

She looks him squarely in the face and says, "If we use the funeral home that my mom's family uses, I'll pay. If not, y'all can figure it out." She turns around and walks off.

Kevin and the remaining children are left scrambling to pay for the funeral. The first place they went for resources was GoFundMe.com.

Unbelievable, right? I try to tell people that their relatives will stay behind after they pass and start *clowning*! There is nothing that can be done. Tracy takes that money and runs for the hills, likely spending it before the next quarter.

HOW TO AVOID THIS

You should know the drill by now. Whatever Bill did, he should not have named Tracy the sole beneficiary on the insurance policy. First, he did not intend for all the money to go to Tracy, even if she partially followed his wishes and at least paid to bury him.

Bill could have set up a trust and named it as the beneficiary on the life insurance policy. The trust terms could've dictated that the money be split equally between the siblings without the need for probate. The other assets could have been placed in the trust as well.

But with this story, the kids were just trying to get Daddy in the ground. At minimum, if Bill did not want to do estate planning, he should have listed all his children as equal beneficiaries on the life insurance policy. This would have put some money in the other children's hands, and they could have paid for the funeral service without starting a GoFundMe campaign.

CHAPTER 8

STEPMONSTER

Tommy married young and has one child. He is a mechanical engineer and ultimately becomes a professor. He provides a good life for his wife, Jill, and son, Tommy Jr.

Years goes by, and Tommy Jr. gets married, moves out of state, and eventually has children. Tommy Sr. and Jill decide to go online and download templates for estate planning documents. In Tommy Sr.'s Will, he names Jill as his Personal Representative or Executor. He leaves his property to Jill and has some provisions in place for Tommy Jr. and his children before they reach a certain age.

One day, Jill is at home straightening up. She is trying to take the basket of laundry upstairs and can barely pull up the steps without gasping for air. She has been out of breath a lot lately. Tommy Sr. insists on taking her to the hospital. At the hospital, the doctors run several tests. It's later determined that Jill has an exorbitant amount of fluid in her lungs. Oncology is notified, and it turns out that Jill has lung cancer, which explains the fluid.

Ten months later, despite the treatment, Jill passes away at sixty-two years old. Tommy Sr. is devastated, understandably so. They had been married for forty-two years. He attempts to move on with his life, realizing his son and grandkids are out of state, and he is all alone. He needs to pick up some new hobbies to keep himself busy. He starts going to the gym, where he ultimately meets Catherine at the smoothie bar.

Catherine is a very attractive young woman, who is twenty-five years Tommy Sr.'s junior. She is a yoga instructor at the gym. Tommy starts spending a lot of time with Catherine, who he knows is much younger than him and doesn't have much, but she makes him feel alive again.

Catherine starts spending a lot of time with Tommy Sr.

Tommy Sr.'s accounts were solely owned. So, the representatives at these institutions will only speak with his son if he opens an estate in probate court.

at the house that he previously shared with Jill for decades. Tommy Jr. gets wind of the budding relationship and writes it off as his dad going through a crisis, assuming it will pass. Boy, is he wrong!

One day, Tommy Jr.'s phone rings and it's his dad. He tells him, "Son, I've got some news to tell you. Catherine and I got married down at the courthouse today."

Tommy Jr. is speechless. He had only known Catherine for a few months. He talks to his wife, Laura, about planning a trip home with the kids to check on his dad and then have the difficult conversation about his affairs, given his new young, blushing bride. The trip never happens. Tommy Jr. has to go to Europe for work instead.

While he's in Europe, Tommy Jr. talks to his dad, who says he hasn't been feeling well. Tommy Jr. tells his dad to have Catherine take him to the hospital, but being the stubborn guy he is, Tommy Sr. doesn't want to go. Three days later, Catherine finally takes him to the hospital. Tommy Sr. goes into cardiac arrest and passes away—twenty days after he and Catherine tied the knot.

Tommy Jr. takes the long trek home to bury his dad. He finds his dad's Will, which was completed when his mom was still alive, and sees that his mom is still named as his spouse and listed as a beneficiary. He begins placing calls to banks and life insurance companies and discovers that no one will give him information because, after his mom passed, Tommy Sr.'s accounts were solely owned. So, the representatives at these institutions will only speak with his son if he opens an estate in probate court.

Tommy Jr. thinks Catherine, having been married to his dad for such a short period of time, is not entitled to anything. But Tommy Jr. is wrong again. Legally, Catherine is Tommy Sr.'s spouse. And although it was a surprising decision, Tommy was in his right mind when he chose to marry Catherine, so there is no way to get the marriage invalidated.

As a surviving spouse, by law, Catherine is entitled to a portion of Tommy's Sr.'s assets, despite the Will naming the first wife who passed away. Tommy Jr. is completely blown away and devastated. He doesn't understand how a woman who had only been married to his dad for twenty days and whom he had only met a few months ago is entitled to anything.

Tommy Jr. hires a lawyer to open the estate and sell all his dad's possessions. This leaves cash in the estate, and Catherine receives a nice chunk. The home is worth $750,000, and Tommy Sr. has bank accounts with about $300,000 in them. Catherine, as the legal spouse, is also entitled to the 401k, which has a balance of around $375,000.

HOW TO AVOID THIS

After Jill passed away, Tommy should have updated his estate plan. He could have used a trust, which is a handy tool when you want to provide for a new spouse and children from a previous relationship. Had Tommy Sr. set this up and put his assets in the trust, Tommy Jr. would've avoided probate court, and he would have been able to control exactly what Catherine received.

CHAPTER 9

MILLION DOLLAR BABY

S amantha is a twenty-three-year-old single mother with a three-year-old son, Charlie. She graduates from college and gets a good job with a national bank. While Samantha does not have a lot of assets, she knows she wants to always be able to care for her son. She decides to get a life insurance policy.

It takes a while to go through underwriting, as Samantha has a heart condition, but ultimately, she completes the process and the policy is issued. The death benefit is $1,000,000, and she names Charlie as the beneficiary. God forbid, if something happens to her, Charlie is set. She is proud of herself.

Things seem to be going well for Samantha. She feels like she's gotten to a point where her health is stable, and she is advancing at work. Samantha is close with her mother,

Joyce, who often helps out with Charlie. Charlie's dad—whom Samantha was never married to—is in jail, so she can't count on him.

One day, while at work, Samantha feels a little flushed. She gets up to walk to the bathroom and collapses. Her coworker calls 9-1-1. Samantha is rushed to the hospital and hooked to a ventilator. The prognosis is not good.

A week later, Joyce makes the difficult decision no one ever wants to make—to remove Samantha from life-sustaining treatment. Joyce keeps her strength, knowing Charlie has no one but her now. Joyce must go to probate court

It means she will have to go back to probate court and be appointed as conservator to manage the funds for Charlie. She will be subject to public proceedings, annual accountings, constant court involvement to get approval for access to the funds, and worst of all, she must notify Charlie's dad of the proceedings.

to get guardianship over Charlie, which will allow Joyce to stand in the shoes of his parent, arrange for his medical care, and enroll him in school. Since Charlie's dad is still in jail and his other grandmother is not interested in taking him in, that process is relatively smooth.

Joyce calls the agent who set up Samantha's insurance policy. She plans on getting the funds and investing most of them, leaving some behind to take care of regular expenses for Charlie. The agent tells Joyce the insurance company is requiring that she open a conservatorship. Since Samantha named Charlie—a minor—as the beneficiary, it is required.

Joyce can barely say the word "conservatorship," let alone understand what it means. It means she will have to go back to probate court and be appointed as conservator to manage the funds for Charlie. She will be subject to public proceedings, annual accountings, constant court involvement to get approval for access to the funds, and worst of all, she must notify Charlie's dad of the proceedings.

Joyce is sick to her stomach. Although Charlie's dad was ultimately released from jail, he is living in Arizona with a random cousin and still up to his old tricks. However, he is still Charlie's dad and has priority over Joyce to manage money for Charlie. Nobody, on their worst and drunkest day, wants this. But it is reality.

Joyce must prove Charlie's dad is unfit to serve due to his transient lifestyle and criminal past, which includes theft. Several months later, with thousands of dollars spent on attorney's fees, Joyce is finally appointed as conservator.

HOW TO AVOID THIS

You probably know the answer by now. If you have minor children, you need a trust *and* to make sure the assets end up there. If Samantha had a trust, named the trust as beneficiary of the life insurance policy, and named Joyce as the one who would manage the money for Charlie, Joyce would have been able to avoid conservatorship altogether. Charlie's dad would not have priority to serve as trustee of Samantha's trust. In simple terms, this means that Samantha's choice for whom she wanted to manage money for Charlie would've been honored without the need for court involvement or any say from Charlie's father.

CLOSING

Caregiving, navigating sick loved ones, and grief are incredibly stressful. Why would you want to add the unpredictability of a probate process to it? Even in situations where all relatives get along or perhaps there is no relative to argue with, probate court is costly, time consuming, and public.

The good thing is that probate court *is* avoidable—if you take the time to invest and have your estate plan done by a competent estate planning attorney. This is not a practice area to dabble in. So as amazing as your cousin Buddy's daughter is, if she only practices criminal law, she need not be drafting your estate plan. A skilled estate planning attorney knows how to plan for the unexpected, can walk you through the implications of your decisions, and knows how to put together a plan that addresses your unique needs concerning your specific assets and your loved ones.

A do-it-yourself plan is also risky. You may not understand the implications in the language on the forms you print from the internet. It could become a one-way ticket to probate court.

Wayne County Probate Court is the busiest probate court

in the State of Michigan, handling over 38,000 hearings and over 13,500 new filings per year. There is an active case docket of over 33,000 cases! This is *one* county, in *one* state alone. In contrast, there are limited staff to handle this high volume. And that leads to delays! So, in addition to the other woes of probate court, you can expect *time* to be another major factor. Probate courts across the country would not be nearly as busy if we changed our mindset on things.

Sure, no one loves to talk about their mortality, but the reality is death is a part of life. Just like you plan for vacations, weddings, babies, graduations, moves, changing jobs, anniversaries, and retirement, you must plan for sickness and death. I know, I know, it *is* morbid (my dad calls me the grim reaper attorney and tells me no one wants to see me coming), but wouldn't you prefer to have the uncomfortable conversations and have a solid plan rather than having your loved ones go through a stressful public process, only for a probate judge to make decisions you could have made for yourself? I like to think the answer to that long, drawn-out question is yes.

So, do the right thing. Get your affairs in order. Start with identifying your "what," "who," and "how." Your "what" means what assets you have, whether you only have a bank account and a car or multiple businesses, retirement accounts, and properties. Your "who" consists of two parts: who you want to handle your healthcare and financial decisions if you become unable *and* who you want to leave your assets to. Your "how" is how those individuals will receive what you leave behind if you want to put parameters on it or make sure the most vulnerable are fully protected, i.e., children and those with special needs, regardless of their age.

Estate planning is a necessary investment we all need to make. It is literally a matter of life and death.

APPENDICES

ESTATE PLANNING DOCUMENT TEMPLATES

~

These forms are general templates. They are for informational purposes only and should not be construed as legal advice on any subject matter. These forms either have references to Michigan law, provided by the Institute of Continuing Legal Education (ICLE), or the language is included in existing Michigan laws. You should not act or refrain from acting on the basis of any content included in these forms without seeking legal or other professional advice. You should not sign or otherwise rely on these templates without seeking legal or other professional advice. These forms do not create an attorney-client relationship between you and the author or you and Great Lakes Legal Group PLLC.

APPENDIX I

SAMPLE GENERAL (FINANCIAL) POWER OF ATTORNEY

DESIGNATION OF AGENT

I _____ name

(Name of Principal)

the following person as my agent:

Name of Agent: _____

Agent's Address: _____

Agent's Telephone Number: _____

DESIGNATION OF SUCCESSOR AGENT(S)
(OPTIONAL)

If my agent is unable or unwilling to act for me, I name as my successor agent:

Name of Successor Agent: _____

Successor Agent's Address: _____

Successor Agent's Telephone Number: _____

If my successor agent is unable or unwilling to act for me, I name as my second successor agent:

Name of Second Successor Agent: _____

Second Successor Agent's Address: _____

Second Successor Agent's Telephone Number: _____

GRANT OF GENERAL AUTHORITY

I grant my agent and any successor agent general authority to act for me with respect to the following subjects as defined in the uniform power of attorney act, MCL 556.201 to 556.505:

(INITIAL each subject you want to include in the agent's general authority. If you wish to grant general authority over all of the subjects, you may simply initial "All Preceding Subjects.")

(___) Real Property

(___) Tangible Personal Property

(___) Stocks and Bonds

(___) Commodities and Options

(___) Banks and Other Financial Institutions

(___) Operation of Entity or Business

(___) Insurance and Annuities

(___) Estates, Trusts, and Other Beneficial Interests

(___) Claims and Litigation

(___) Personal and Family Maintenance

(___) Benefits from Governmental Programs or Civil or Military Service

(___) Retirement Plans

(___) Taxes

    (___) All Preceding Subjects (regardless of whether any of the preceding subjects are initialed)

GRANT OF SPECIFIC AUTHORITY (OPTIONAL)

My agent MAY NOT do any of the following specific acts for me UNLESS I have INITIALED the specific authority listed below:

CAUTION: Granting any of the following will give your agent the authority to take actions that could significantly reduce your property or change how your property is distributed at your death. Furthermore, depending on the amount in one or more of the accounts mentioned in the last item listed below (which refers to 31 CFR 1010.350), granting that particular power may subject your agent to burdensome federal reporting obligations that are subject to stiff penalties. INITIAL ONLY the specific authority you WANT to give your agent. If you have questions about the wisdom of granting any specific authority to your agent, you should seek legal advice before signing this form. If you are inclined to grant specific authority but doubt the wisdom of granting that authority to a particular person you have designated as your agent or successor agent, you should ask yourself whether you have designated the right person(s).

(___) Create, amend, revoke, or terminate an inter vivos trust

(___) Make a gift as limited by section 217 of the uniform power of attorney act, MCL 556.317, and any special instructions in this power of attorney

(____) Create or change rights of survivorship by, for example, creating a joint account

(____) Create or change a beneficiary designation

(____) Authorize another person to exercise the authority granted under this power of attorney

(____) Waive the principal's right to be a beneficiary of a joint and survivor annuity, including a survivor benefit under a retirement plan

(____) Exercise fiduciary powers that the principal has authority to delegate

(____) Access the content of electronic communications

(____) Exercise authority over any "bank, securities, or other financial account in a foreign country" within the meaning of 31 CFR 1010.350

LIMITATION ON AGENT'S AUTHORITY

Even if I have authorized my agent to make a gift (by initialing the relevant line above), an agent who is not my ancestor, spouse, or descendant MAY NOT use my property to benefit the agent or a person to whom the agent owes an obligation of support unless I have included that authority in the Special Instructions.

SPECIAL INSTRUCTIONS (OPTIONAL)

You may give special instructions on the following lines.

CAUTION! Special instructions are liable to cause ambiguities that may impair the effectiveness of this power of attorney. You are taking a solemn step if you decide to make any use of this form without seeking legal advice; you should be especially wary of providing special instructions without the benefit of legal counsel.

_____

_____

_____

_____

_____

_____

_____

EFFECTIVE DATE

This power of attorney is effective immediately unless I have stated otherwise in the Special Instructions.

EFFECT ON PREVIOUS POWERS OF ATTORNEY

Unless I have said otherwise in the Special Instructions, the execution of this power of attorney does not revoke any prior power of attorney.

NOMINATION OF CONSERVATOR OR GUARDIAN (OPTIONAL)

If it becomes necessary for a court to appoint a conservator or guardian of my estate or guardian of my person, I nominate the following person(s) for appointment:

Name of Nominee for Conservator or Guardian of My Estate:

_____

Nominee's Address: _____

Nominee's Telephone Number: _____

Name of Nominee for Guardian of My Person: _____

Nominee's Address: _____

Nominee's Telephone Number: _____

RELIANCE ON THIS POWER OF ATTORNEY

Any person, including my agent, may rely upon the validity of this power of attorney or a copy of it unless that person knows that the power has terminated or is invalid.

SIGNATURE OF PRINCIPAL, SIGNATURES OF WITNESSES, AND ACKNOWLEDGMENT

CAUTION! Unless you provide otherwise in the Special Instructions, this form will create a "durable" power of attorney if you sign it either before a notary public (or other individual authorized to take acknowledgments) or in the presence of two witnesses neither of whom is designated as your agent or successor agent, both of whom sign below (and one of whom may be the notary public or other individual authorized by law to take acknowledgments who also signs below in his or her official capacity). The power's being "durable" means that unless the power is revoked or the agent's authority is otherwise terminated beforehand, your agent's authority will continue during any period in which you are alive but incapacitated. If you have questions about the wisdom of making this power durable, you should seek legal advice before signing this form.

CAUTION! You have an important motivation to acknowledge your signature before a notary public (or other individual authorized to take acknowledgments) regardless of the question of durability (described above): doing so will make it harder, under section 120 of the uniform power of attorney act, MCL 556.220, for someone to whom the power is presented to decline to accept the power and your agent's authority to act on your behalf.

_____   _____

Your Signature   Date

_____

Your Name Printed

_____

Your Address

_____

Your Telephone Number

_____   _____

Witness No. 1's Signature   Date

_____

Witness No. 1's Name Printed

_____

Witness No. 1's Address

_____   _____

Witness No. 2's Signature Date

_____

Witness No. 2's Name Printed

_____

Witness No. 2's Address

State of _____

[County] of _____

This document was acknowledged before me on _____

                                                        (Date)

by _____.

                    (Name of Principal)

_____ (Seal, if any)

Signature of Notary _____

My commission expires: _____

This document prepared by:

_____

IMPORTANT INFORMATION FOR AGENT

Agent's Duties

When you accept authority granted under this power of attorney, a special legal relationship is created between you and the principal. This relationship imposes upon you legal duties that continue until you resign or the power or your authority under it is terminated by a termination event described in the uniform power of attorney act, MCL 556.201 to 556.505. You must:

(1) Do what you know the principal reasonably expects you to do with the principal's property or, if you do not know the principal's expectations, act in the principal's best interest;

(2) Act in good faith;

(3) Do nothing beyond the authority granted in this power of attorney;

(4) Keep a record of receipts, disbursements, and transactions made on behalf of the principal;

(5) Disclose your identity as an agent whenever you act for the principal by, for example, writing or printing the name of the principal and signing your own name as "agent" in the following manner: (Principal's Name) by (Your Signature) as Agent;

(6) And if the power is "durable" in the sense described below, you must, before acting as agent under the power, sign an

JEHAN CRUMP-GIBSON, ESQ.

acknowledgment of your duties as agent that contains all the declarations contained in the optional template "Agent's Acknowledgment" provided in section 302 of the uniform power of attorney act, MCL 556.402, in substantially the form of that optional template.

Unless the Special Instructions in this power of attorney state otherwise, you must also:

(1) ct loyally for the principal's benefit;
(2) Avoid conflicts that would impair your ability to act in the principal's best interest;
(3) Act with care, competence, and diligence;
(4) Cooperate with any person that has authority to make health care decisions for the principal to do what you know the principal reasonably expects concerning health care or, if you do not know the principal's expectations, to act in the principal's best interest; and
(5) Attempt, to the extent of the powers you have been granted as agent, to preserve the principal's estate plan if you know the plan and preserving the plan is consistent with the principal's best interest.

Termination of Agent's Authority

You must stop acting on behalf of the principal if you learn of any event that terminates this power of attorney or your authority under it. Events that terminate a power of attorney or your authority to act under such a power include:

(1) Death of the principal;
(2) The principal's revocation of the power of attorney or your authority;
(3) The occurrence of a termination event stated in the power;
(4) If the power is intended only for a specified, limited purpose, the specified purpose of the power is fully accomplished; or
(5) If you are married to the principal, a legal action is filed with a court to end your marriage, or for your legal separation, unless the Special Instructions in this power of attorney state that such an action will not terminate your authority.

Statutory Duty to Acknowledge Agent's Duties under "Durable" Power

Unless the Special Instructions in this power of attorney state otherwise, this form will create a "durable" power of attorney (meaning that unless the power is revoked or your authority is otherwise terminated beforehand, your authority as agent will continue during any period in which the principal is alive but incapacitated) if the principal signs it either before a notary public (or other individual authorized to take acknowledgments) or in the presence of two witnesses neither of whom is designated as the principal's agent or successor agent and both of whom also sign the form. If this power of attorney is durable, then before you act as agent under the power, you must execute an acknowledgment of your duties as agent that contains all the declarations contained in the optional template "Agent's Acknowledgment" provided in section 302 of the uniform power of attorney act, MCL 556.402, in substantially the form of that optional template.

Liability of Agent

The meaning of the authority granted to you is defined in the uniform power of attorney act, MCL 556.201 to 556.505. If you violate that act or the terms of this power, you may be liable for any damages caused by your violation.

If there is anything about this document or your duties under it that you do not understand, you should seek legal advice.

AGENT'S ACKNOWLEDGMENT

I, _____, have been appointed agent for
_____ (Your Name), the principal
_____ (Name of Principal),
under a durable power of attorney dated _____.
By signing this document, I acknowledge that if and when I act
as agent under the power, all of the following apply:

MY DUTIES AS AGENT

I must:

1. Do what I know the principal reasonably expects me to
   do with the principal's property or, if I do not know the
   principal's expectations, act in the principal's best interest.
2. Act in good faith.
3. Do nothing beyond the authority granted in the durable
   power of attorney.
4. Keep reasonable records of receipts, disbursements, and
   transactions I make on behalf of the principal.
5. Disclose my identity as an agent whenever I act for the
   principal by writing or printing the principal's name and
   signing my own name as "agent".
6. And depending on the terms of the power of attorney, I
   may have additional duties described in section 114 of the
   uniform power of attorney act, MCL 556.201 to 556.505,

including the presumptive duties to act loyally for the principal's benefit, avoid conflicts of interest that would make it hard for me to act in the principal's best interest, and act with care, competence, and diligence.

POWERS REQUIRING SPECIFIC AUTHORITY

Unless specifically provided in the durable power of attorney or by judicial order, I cannot do any of the following:

1. Create, amend, revoke, or terminate an inter vivos trust.
2. Make a gift of the principal's property to someone else, let alone to myself.
3. Create or change rights of survivorship by, for example, creating a joint account.
4. Create or change a beneficiary designation.
5. Delegate authority granted under the durable power of attorney.
6. Exercise fiduciary powers that the principal has authority to delegate.
7. Waive the principal's right to be a beneficiary of a joint and survivor annuity, including a survivor benefit under a retirement plan.
8. Exercise authority over the content of electronic communications, as defined in 18 USC 2510, sent or received by the principal.

9. Exercise authority over any bank, securities, or other financial account in a foreign country within the meaning of 31 CFR 1010.350.

TERMINATION OF MY AUTHORITY

I must stop acting on behalf of the principal if I learn of any event that terminates the durable power of attorney or my authority under the power, including the death of the principal or the principal's revocation of either the power or my authority to act under it.

MY POTENTIAL LIABILITY AS AGENT

If I violate the uniform power of attorney act, MCL 556.201 to 556.505, or act outside the authority granted in the durable power, I may be liable to the principal or the principal's successors for damages caused by my violation and to civil or criminal penalties. An exoneration clause in the power (if any) does not relieve me of liability for acts or omissions committed in bad faith or, in some cases, for acts or omissions committed with reckless indifference to the purposes of the power of attorney or the interests of the principal.

Signature: _____ Date: _____

CERTIFICATION AS TO THE VALIDITY OF POWER OF ATTORNEY AND AGENT'S AUTHORITY

State of _____

[County] of _____

I, _____ (Name of Certifier), certify under penalty of perjury that

_____ (Name of Principal) granted

_____ (Name of Agent)

authority as an agent or successor agent in a power of attorney dated _____ .

I further certify that to my knowledge:

(1) The Principal is alive and has not revoked the Power of Attorney or the Agent's authority to act under the Power and the Power and the Agent's authority to act under the Power have not otherwise terminated;

(2) If the Power of Attorney was drafted to become effective upon the happening of a specified event or contingency, the specified event or contingency has occurred;

(3) If the Agent was named as a successor agent, the prior agent is unable or unwilling to serve; and

(4) _____

_____

(Insert other relevant statements. You may attach separate sheets if additional space is needed.)

SIGNATURE AND ACKNOWLEDGMENT

_____   _____
Certifier's Signature   Date

_____
Certifier's Name Printed

_____
Certifier's Capacity (as Agent, attorney at law for Agent, or attorney at law for Principal)

_____
Certifier's Address

_____
Certifier's Telephone Number

This document was acknowledged before me on _____,

                                                     (Date)

by _____.

                    (Name of Certifier)

_____ (Seal, if any)
Signature of Notary

My commission expires: _____

This document prepared by:

_____

_____

SAMPLE LIVING TRUST FOR UNMARRIED PERSON

THE JANE DOE LIVING TRUST

Establishing My Trust

The date of this trust is [date]. The parties to this trust are Jane Doe (*Settlor*) and Jane Doe a/k/a (*Trustee*).

I intend to create a valid trust under the laws of Michigan and under the laws of any state in which any trust created under this trust document is administered. The terms of this trust prevail over any provision of Michigan law, except those provisions that are mandatory and may not be waived.

Identifying My Trust

To the extent practicable, for the purpose of transferring property to my trust or identifying my trust in any beneficiary or pay-on-death designation, my trust should be identified as:

> "Jane Doe, Trustee, or her successors in interest, of the Jane Doe Living Trust dated [date], and any amendments thereto."

Transferring Property to My Trust

By executing this instrument, I transfer, convey, and assign to my Trustee the trust property described in the attached Schedule A. I also transfer, convey, and assign to my Trustee all of my real and personal property that is permitted by law to be held in trust, wherever situated and whether tangible or intangible, unless specifically reserved as having not been transferred to the trust. My Trustee accepts and agrees to hold the property transferred to the trust as trust property. My Trustee must accept any additional property transferred to my trust before it becomes part of the trust property. My Trustee shall hold, administer, and dispose of all accepted trust property for my benefit and for the benefit of my beneficiaries, in accordance with the terms of this instrument.

Powers Reserved by Me as Settlor

As Settlor, I retain the powers set forth in this Section in addition to any powers that I reserve in other provisions of this instrument.

Action on Behalf of My Trust

> Whenever I am serving as Trustee, I may act for and conduct business on behalf of my trust without the consent of any other Trustee.

Amendment, Restatement, or Revocation

I may amend, restate, or revoke this instrument, in whole or in part, for any purpose. Any amendment, restatement, or revocation must be made in writing and delivered to the then-serving Trustee.

Addition or Removal of Trust Property

I may add property to my trust and may remove any property from my trust at any time.

Control of Income and Principal Distributions

I retain the right to control the distribution of income and principal from my trust. I may direct my Trustee to distribute as much of the net income and principal of the trust property as I consider advisable to me or to other persons or entities. My Trustee may distribute the net income and principal to me or for my unrestricted use and benefit, even to the exhaustion of all trust property. Any undistributed net income is to be added to the principal of my trust.

Approval of Investment Decisions

> I reserve the absolute right to review and change my Trustee's investment decisions. But my Trustee is not required to seek my approval before making investment decisions.

Family Information

I am unmarried. I have the following children: _____[name of child]. Any references to child or children refer to this child only.

Trustee Succession

Resignation of a Trustee

A Trustee may resign by giving written notice to me. If I am incapacitated or deceased, a Trustee may resign by giving written notice to the trust's current income beneficiaries and to any Co-Trustees.

Trustee Succession

This Section governs the removal and replacement of my Trustees.

My Right to Remove and Replace Trustees

During my lifetime and during any period I am not incapacitated, I may remove any Trustee with or without cause at any time. If a Trustee is removed, resigns, or cannot continue to serve for any reason, I may serve as sole Trustee, name a Trustee to serve with me, or name a successor Trustee.

Successor Trustees

Upon my incapacity or death, I name the following to serve as successor Trustee, in the order named, replacing any then-serving Trustee:

[successor trustee name]

Removal and Replacement of Trustees

After my death or incapacity, a majority of the income beneficiaries of any trust created under this instrument may remove a Trustee of the trust, with or without cause.

A Trustee may be removed under this Subsection only if the person with the right of removal names an individual or a corporate fiduciary that simultaneously begins service as Trustee by the effective removal date.

If the office of Trustee of a trust created under this instrument is vacant and no designated successor Trustee is able and willing to act as Trustee, a majority of the income beneficiaries may name a successor Trustee.

Incapacity of a Trustee

If any individual Trustee becomes incapacitated, the incapacitated Trustee need not resign as Trustee. For Trustees other than me, a written, good-faith declaration of incapacity by the Co-Trustee or, if none, by the party designated to succeed the incapacitated Trustee, will terminate the trusteeship. If the Trustee designated in the written declaration objects in writing to termination of the trusteeship within five days of receiving the declaration of incapacity, a written opinion of incapacity signed by a physician who has examined this Trustee must be obtained before the trusteeship will be terminated for incapacity. The Trustee objecting to termination of trusteeship must sign the necessary medical releases needed to obtain the physician's written opinion of incapacity, or the trusteeship will be terminated without the physician's written opinion.

JEHAN CRUMP-GIBSON, ESQ.

Documenting Change of Trustee Status

Any appointment, removal, resignation, or other change in trusteeship must be in writing and signed by the person or persons exercising the power. The written notice must be dated, must specify the effective date and other terms regarding the change of Trustee status, and must be delivered as specified in Section 3.05 of this instrument.

Notice of Removal and Appointment

Notice of removal must be delivered to the Trustee being removed, and to any other then-serving Trustees. The notice of removal will be effective in accordance with its provisions.

Notice of appointment must be delivered to the successor Trustee and any other then-serving Trustees. The appointment will become effective at the time of acceptance by the successor Trustee. A copy of the notice of appointment may be attached to this instrument.

Administration of My Trust during My Incapacity

During any period of time when I am incapacitated, my Trustee shall administer my trust as provided in this Article.

Distributions for My Benefit

My Trustee shall regularly and conscientiously make appropriate distributions of the net income and principal for my general welfare and comfort under the circumstances existing at the time those distributions are made. My Trustee may make distributions for my benefit in any one or more of the following ways:

> to me, to the extent I am able to manage these distributions;
>
> to other persons and entities for my use and benefit;
>
> to an agent or attorney in fact authorized to act for me under a legally valid durable power of attorney executed by me prior to incapacity; and
>
> to my guardian or conservator, who has assumed responsibility for me under any court order, decree, or judgment issued by a court of competent jurisdiction.

Distributions for the Benefit of My Dependents

My Trustee may distribute as much of the net income and principal as my Trustee considers necessary for the health, education, maintenance, or support of persons that my Trustee determines to be dependent on me for support.

Guidance for Making Distributions

When making distributions under Section 4.01 and Section 4.02, my Trustee shall give consideration first to my needs and then to the needs of those persons dependent on me.

When making distributions under Section 4.02, I request that my Trustee, with sole and absolute discretion, consider other income and resources available to the beneficiaries. My Trustee may make unequal distributions, distributions to some but not all beneficiaries, or no distributions.

A distribution made to a beneficiary under this Section will not be considered an advancement, and will not be charged against the share of the beneficiary that may be distributable under any other provision of this instrument.

Administration of My Trust upon My Death

Payment of Expenses and Taxes

After my death, my Trustee may pay from the trust property:

expenses of my last illness, funeral, and burial or cremation, including expenses of memorials and memorial services;

legally enforceable claims against me or my estate;

expenses of administering the trust and my estate; and

court-ordered allowances for those dependent upon me.

These payments are discretionary with my Trustee. My Trustee may make decisions on these payments without regard to any limitation on payment of the expenses and may make payments without any court's approval. No third party may enforce any claim or right to payment against the trust by virtue of this discretionary authority.

Payment of Death Taxes

For the purposes of this Article, the term *death taxes* refers to any taxes imposed by reason of my death by federal, state, or local authorities, including estate, inheritance, gift, and direct-skip generation-skipping transfer taxes. For purposes of this Section, *death taxes* does not include any additional estate tax imposed by Internal Revenue Code Section 2031(c)

(5)(C), Section 2032A(c), or any other comparable recapture tax imposed by any taxing authority. Nor does the term include any generation-skipping transfer tax, other than a direct-skip generation-skipping transfer tax.

Except as otherwise specified in this Article or elsewhere in this trust, my Trustee shall apportion and pay death taxes as provided under the laws of Michigan in effect on the date of my death.

Disposition of Tangible Personal Property

Distribution of Tangible Personal Property by Memorandum

I may dispose of items of tangible personal property by a signed written memorandum executed after I sign this instrument. The memorandum must refer to my Trust and must reasonably identify the items and the beneficiary designated to receive each item. If I execute a memorandum, my Trustee shall incorporate the memorandum by reference into this instrument to the extent permitted by law.

My Trustee shall distribute the items of tangible personal property listed in the memorandum as promptly as practicable after my death, together with any insurance policies covering the property and any claims under those policies, as provided in the memorandum. If I leave multiple written memoranda that conflict as to the disposition of any item of tangible personal property, the memorandum with the most recent date will control as to that item.

If the law does not permit incorporation of the memorandum by reference, the memorandum will then serve as an amendment to my trust, but only to the extent this amendment solely disposes of tangible personal property. I request that my Trustee follow my wishes and distribute the items of tangible personal property listed in a memorandum according to its terms.

Distribution of Tangible Personal Property

My Trustee shall divide and distribute my tangible personal property to my child. If my child does not survive me or dies before distribution is complete, then my Trustee shall divide and distribute my tangible personal property to my siblings in, as nearly equal shares as possible. If there is a dispute among my beneficiaries over which items of tangible personal property each is to receive, Trustee shall determine final distribution of those items. If an item is more appropriate for distribution at a later date, it may be held by Trustee and be delivered to the beneficiary when Trustee deems best.

Until property distributed in accordance with this Article is delivered to the appropriate beneficiary or the beneficiary's

Legal Representative, my Trustee shall pay the reasonable expenses of securing, storing, insuring, packing, transporting, and otherwise caring for the property as an administration expense. Except as otherwise provided in my trust, my Trustee shall distribute property under this Article subject to all liens, security interests, and other encumbrances on the property.

Distribution to My Beneficiaries

Balance of Property

Trustee shall distribute all other trust assets to my child as follows:

> **(a) Distribution.** Each share shall constitute a Separate Trust to be administered as provided below. Trustee, however, shall pay to the beneficiary the amount, if any, that the beneficiary is then entitled to receive and decides to withdraw.

> **(b) Identification of trusts.** To facilitate identification, Trustee shall designate each Separate Trust with the name of the beneficiary for whom it was established.

Separate Trusts

Income. Trustee may distribute net income or may accumulate income of a Separate Trust or add it to principal. The distribution of current and accumulated income is governed by the provisions that authorize use of principal.

Principal. Trustee may distribute principal to the beneficiary (even to the exhaustion of the Separate Trust) in Trustee's discretion to provide for the beneficiary's health, education, support, and maintenance in the beneficiary's accustomed manner of living provide or provide funds for the beneficiary's best interests. When making distributions under this section, Trustee shall have no duty to consider other resources available to the distributee, but may do so if Trustee deems it advisable.

Age Withdrawal. At which time the beneficiary attains age 25, the beneficiary has a continuing right to withdraw the balance of **all trust assets**. The amount subject to withdrawal shall be computed on the date the beneficiary attains the specified age or, if later, the date of the creation of the Separate Trust. The computations shall assume that prior unexercised withdrawals were fully exercised and removed from the trust.

Contingent Distribution

If my child predeceases me or dies before distribution is complete, then Trustee shall divide and distribute the remainder of all trust assets to my siblings in equal shares, outright and free of trust. If at any time no person or entity is qualified to receive final distribution of any part of my trust estate, that portion of my trust estate must be distributed to those persons who would inherit it had I then died intestate owning the property, as determined and proportioned under the laws of Michigan then in effect.

Distributions to Underage and Incapacitated Beneficiaries

If my Trustee is authorized or directed under any provision of this trust to distribute net income or principal to a person who has not yet reached 18 years of age or who is incapacitated as defined in Section 11.05, my Trustee may make the distribution by any one or more of the methods described in Section 9.01, if specific provisions in Article 7 are not applicable.

I request that before making a distribution to a beneficiary, my Trustee consider, to the extent reasonable, the ability the beneficiary has demonstrated in managing prior distributions of trust property.

Methods of Distribution

My Trustee may distribute trust property for any beneficiary's benefit, subject to the provisions of this Article in any one or more of the following methods:

> My Trustee may distribute trust property directly to the beneficiary.

> My Trustee may distribute trust property to the beneficiary's guardian, conservator, parent, other family member, or any person who has assumed the responsibility of caring for the beneficiary.

> My Trustee may distribute trust property to any person or entity, including my Trustee, as custodian for the beneficiary under the Uniform Transfers to Minors Act or similar statute.

> My Trustee may distribute trust property to other persons and entities for the beneficiary's use and benefit.

> My Trustee may distribute trust property to an agent or attorney in fact authorized to act for the beneficiary under a valid durable power of attorney executed by the beneficiary before becoming incapacitated.

Application of Article

Any decision made by my Trustee under this Article is final, controlling, and binding upon all beneficiaries subject to the provisions of this Article.

The provisions of this Article do not apply to distributions to me from any trust established under this trust.

Trust Administration and Trustee Powers

The terms of this trust prevail over any provision of Michigan law, except those provisions that are mandatory and may not be waived.

Distributions to Beneficiaries

Whenever this instrument authorizes or directs my Trustee to make a distribution of net income or principal to a beneficiary, my Trustee may apply any property that otherwise could be distributed directly to the beneficiary for the beneficiary's benefit. My Trustee does not have a duty to inquire into the beneficiary's ultimate disposition of the distributed property unless specifically directed otherwise by this instrument.

Trustee Compensation

Except for any Settlor, an individual serving as Trustee is entitled to fair and reasonable compensation for the services provided as a fiduciary and to be reimbursed for reasonable expenses incurred in carrying out the Trustee's duties under this instrument. A Trustee may charge additional fees for services the Trustee provides that are not comprised within the duties as Trustee, including fees for legal services, tax return preparation, and corporate finance or investment banking services.

Determination of Principal and Income

The Michigan Principal and Income Law will govern beneficiaries' rights among themselves in matters concerning principal and income. If the Michigan Principal and Income Law contains no provision concerning a particular item, my Trustee will determine in an equitable and practical manner what will be credited, charged, and apportioned between principal and income.

Reports

Whenever I am not serving as Trustee, the Trustee of each trust created under this instrument shall prepare an annual report showing the receipts, disbursements, and distributions of income, principal, and the assets on hand. The Trustee shall deliver the report to the income beneficiary unless the beneficiary waives the right to the annual report. Delivery of a federal fiduciary income tax return filed for the trust will satisfy the annual report requirement of this Section for the year of the return.

My Trustee's Powers

My Trustee may exercise all the powers conferred by this instrument without prior approval from any court, and may perform every act reasonably necessary to administer my trust estate as established under this instrument. My Trustee may also exercise any powers conferred by law, including all those powers set forth under the common law or statutory laws of Michigan or any other jurisdiction whose laws apply to this trust. The powers set forth in the Michigan Estate and Protected Individuals Code are specifically incorporated into this instrument. The powers conferred upon my Trustee by law, including those powers conferred by the Michigan Estate and Protected Individuals Code, are to be subject to any express limitations or contrary directions contained in this instrument.

My Trustee shall exercise these powers in the manner my Trustee determines to be in the beneficiaries' best interests. My Trustee may not exercise any of my Trustee's powers in a manner that is inconsistent with the beneficiaries' right to the beneficial enjoyment of the trust property in accordance with the general principles of the law of trusts. A Trustee of a trust may have duties and responsibilities in addition to those described in this instrument. I encourage my Trustee to obtain appropriate legal advice if my Trustee has any questions concerning the duties and responsibilities as Trustee.

General Provisions

Maximum Term for Trusts

Notwithstanding any other provision of my trust to the contrary, unless terminated earlier under other provisions of my trust, each trust created under my trust will terminate 21 years after the last to die of the descendants of my maternal and paternal grandparents, who are living at the time of my death.

At that time, the remaining trust property will vest in and be distributed to the persons entitled to receive mandatory distributions of net income of the trust and in the same proportions. If no beneficiary is entitled to mandatory distributions of net income, the remaining trust property will vest in and be distributed to the beneficiaries entitled to receive discretionary distributions of net income of the trust, in equal shares *by representation*.

Spendthrift Provision

No beneficiary of any trust created under this trust may assign, anticipate, encumber, alienate, or otherwise voluntarily transfer the income or principal of any trust created under this trust. In addition, neither the income nor the principal of any trust created under this trust is subject to attachment, bankruptcy proceedings or any other legal process, the interference or control of creditors or others, or any involuntary transfer.

This Section does not restrict a beneficiary's right to disclaim any interest or exercise of any power of appointment granted in this trust.

Contest Provision

If any person directly or indirectly attempts to contest or oppose the validity of my trust, or commences, continues, or prosecutes any legal proceedings to set my trust aside, then that person will forfeit his or her share, cease to have any right or interest in the trust property, and will, for purposes of my trust, be deemed to have predeceased me.

Survivorship Presumption

If any beneficiary is living at my death, but dies within 30 days after my death, then the beneficiary will be considered to have predeceased me.

Incapacity

Except as otherwise provided in this instrument, a person is considered incapacitated in any of the following circumstances.

The Opinion of Two Licensed Physicians

An individual is considered to be incapacitated whenever two licensed physicians give the opinion that the individual is unable to effectively manage his or her property or financial affairs, whether as a result of age; illness; use of prescription medications, drugs, or other substances; or any other cause. If an individual whose capacity is in question refuses to provide necessary documentation or otherwise submit to examination by licensed physicians, that individual will be considered incapacitated.

An individual is considered restored to capacity whenever the individual's personal or attending physician provides a written opinion that the individual is able to effectively manage his or her property and financial affairs.

Court Determination

An individual is considered incapacitated if a court of competent jurisdiction has declared the individual to be disabled, incompetent, or legally incapacitated.

General Provisions and Rules of Construction

The following general provisions and rules of construction apply to this trust.

Multiple Originals; Validity of Paper or Electronic Copies

This trust may be executed in any number of counterparts, each of which will be considered an original.

Any person may rely on a paper or electronic copy of this trust that the Trustee certifies to be a true copy as if it were an original.

Singular and Plural; Gender

Unless the context requires otherwise, singular words may be construed as plural, and plural words may be construed as singular. Words of one gender may be construed as denoting another gender as is appropriate within the context. The word *or,* when used in a list of more than two items, may function as both a conjunction and a disjunction as the context requires.

Headings of Articles, Sections, and Subsections

The headings of Articles, Sections, and Subsections used within this trust are included solely for the convenience of the reader. They have no significance in the interpretation or construction of this trust.

Governing State Law

This trust is governed, construed, and administered according to the laws of Michigan, as amended except as to trust property required by law to be governed by the laws of another jurisdiction and unless the situs of administration is changed pursuant to Michigan law.

Notices

Unless otherwise stated, any notice required under this trust will be in writing. The notice may be personally delivered with proof of delivery to the party requiring notice and will be effective on the date personally delivered. Notice may also be mailed, postage prepaid, by certified mail with return receipt requested to the last known address of the party requiring notice. Mailed notice is effective on the date of the return receipt. If a party giving notice does not receive the return receipt but has proof that he or she mailed the notice, notice will be effective on the date it would normally have been received via certified mail. If the party requiring notice is a minor or incapacitated individual, notice will be given to the parent or Legal Representative.

Severability

The invalidity or unenforceability of any provision of this trust does not affect the validity or enforceability of any other provision of this trust. If a court of competent jurisdiction determines that any provision is invalid, the remaining provisions of this trust are to be interpreted as if the invalid provision had never been included.

I have executed this trust on [date]. This trust instrument is effective when signed by me, whether or not now signed by a Trustee.

I certify that I have read and understand this trust instrument, and that it correctly states the provisions under which my trust property is to be administered and distributed by my Trustee.

_____

Jane Doe, Settlor and Trustee

STATE OF MICHIGAN)

) ss.

COUNTY OF OAKLAND)

Acknowledged by Jane Doe, as Settlor and as Trustee before me on _____, 20___.

_____

Notary public, State of Michigan,

County of Oakland

My commission expires:

STATE OF MICHIGAN)

) ss.

COUNTY OF OAKLAND)

I, Jane Doe, declare to the officer taking my acknowledgment of this instrument and to the subscribing witnesses that I signed this instrument as my trust.

_____

Jane Doe, Settlor

We, _____ and _____,

have been sworn by the officer signing below, and declare to that officer on our oaths that the Settlor declared the instrument to be the Settlor's trust and signed it in our presence. We each signed the instrument as a witness in the presence of the Settlor and of each other.

_____

_____, Witness

_____

_____, Witness

Schedule A

Ten Dollars cash

_____

_____

_____

_____

_____

_____

_____

_____

_____

_____

_____

_____

_____

_____

_____

_____

_____

_____

_____

_____

_____

_____

_____

_____

_____

SAMPLE LIVING TRUST FOR MARRIED COUPLE

THE DOE FAMILY TRUST

We, Spouse 1 and Spouse 2, hereby adopt and agree to be bound by the terms and provisions of this Trust Agreement established on [date]. We hereby designate ourselves, Spouse 1 and Spouse 2, or the survivor, acting jointly or independently, as Trustee.

Article I. Statement of Name and Purpose

1.1 This Trust shall be known as Doe Family Trust. We have established this Trust as a part of a plan to benefit ourselves, our children, Child 1 and Child 2, including any child born to or adopted by us subsequent to this date, and other persons as provided in this Trust.

Article II. Trust Property

2.1 We hereby transfer, assign, and convey to the Trustee certain property. That property and any other property that may be received by the Trustee shall be held and disposed of in accordance with all of the provisions of this Agreement and shall be referred to as the "principal."

Article III. Rights We Have Reserved During Our Lifetime

3.1 Modification and Revocation. Each of us reserves the right during our lifetime and the lifetime of the survivor to modify or revoke this Trust in whole or in part by an instrument in writing signed by either or both of us if we are both alive and competent, by one of us if one of us has been determined incapacitated by the terms of the Trust, or by the survivor of us.

3.2 Investment Responsibility If We Are Not Acting as Trustee. The Trustee shall make no sale or investment without the written consent and approval of either of us during our lifetimes and the written consent and approval of the survivor during the survivor's lifetime. We also retain the right to designate in writing other persons who may exercise consent, or we may elect in writing to eliminate the necessity of consent. If Trustee, on receipt of at least two physicians' statements, considers that both of us are incapacitated or that the survivor is incapacitated so as to be unable to manage our financial affairs, we waive the requirement of our written consent in order to deal with Trust assets. If one of us becomes incapacitated, the Trustee shall seek written consent from the other.

Article IV. Distribution Provisions

4.1 Assets in Trust During Our Lifetimes. During our lifetimes, and the lifetime of the survivor, we may withdraw the income and principal from the Trust.

(a) If at any time during our lifetimes we should become incapacitated or for any reason be unable to act on our own behalf, the Trustee may, in its absolute discretion, pay to or apply for our benefit or the benefit of any person dependent on us, giving preference to us, such amounts from the income and principal as the Trustee considers to be for our best interests so as to continue the standard of living to which we are accustomed (and, regarding care, custody, and treatment decisions, in consultation with our patient advocates, if any are acting as such). The Trustee shall have the authority, on receipt of at least two physicians' statements, to determine our competence or incompetence, and no liability shall arise against the Trustee as a consequence of the determination.

(b) On either or both of our deaths, the Trustee shall pay out of income or principal the expenses of our last illness and funeral (in consultation with our funeral representatives, if any are acting as such) and all inheritance, estate, and succession taxes, including interest and penalties payable by reason of our deaths to the extent that these items should not be paid or responsibility for their payment is assumed by some other person or estate. The Trustee may also pay out of income or principal, in its sole discretion, all or any portion of the cost of ancillary administration and similar proceedings in other jurisdictions.

4.2 After the Deaths of *Spouse 1* and *Spouse 2*. After the deaths of Spouse 1 and Spouse 2, the Trust shall be irrevocable and administered and disposed of as follows:

4.2A Tangible personal property. We give all of our tangible personal property not otherwise disposed of, such as household furnishings, jewelry, clothing, automobiles, furniture, china, silver, crystal, artwork, collectibles, appliances, equipment, tools, books, cemetery plots, and safe-deposit boxes, to our children who survive us in shares of substantially equal value. While this gift is unrestricted, it is our direction that any memorandum we may leave at our deaths concerning the above-mentioned property be followed by the Trustee

If any child of ours entitled to a share is a minor at the time of distribution, the child's guardian shall represent the child and receipt for. The guardian shall deliver the share or sale proceeds to the child on or before attaining legal age, as the guardian deems to be in the best interests of the child.

4.2B Trust Assets. All remaining assets comprising the Trust shall be divided into as many equal shares as necessary to allot one share to each of our children then surviving and one share for each of our children then deceased who have issue surviving. If a child of ours is not then surviving and leaves no then surviving issue, the share shall lapse. Any share allocated for the benefit of the then surviving issue of our deceased child shall be further divided into per stirpes shares. All shares shall be administered and disposed of as follows:

1. Until a beneficiary attains age 30, the Trustee may pay to the beneficiary or expend on the beneficiary's behalf as much of the income derived from the share as the Trustee, in its sole discretion, may deem advisable to provide properly for the beneficiary's health, education, support, and maintenance. Any income not disbursed shall be added to the principal. If the income and other funds available are insufficient for the beneficiary's health, education, support, and maintenance, the Trustee may pay or apply as much or all of the principal as the Trustee, in its sole discretion, deems necessary.

2. Except as restricted below, after attaining age 25, a beneficiary may withdraw at any time or times a total of one-half of the trust share. The value of the amount that may be withdrawn shall be determined as of the date when the right could first be exercised. Payments shall be made without question on the beneficiary's written request; however, the Trustee may delay honoring a beneficiary's request, if, in the sole discretion of the Trustee, the delay is appropriate due to the then current medical, physical, financial, or emotional problems of the beneficiary. The right of withdrawal shall be a privilege that

may be exercised only voluntarily and shall not include an involuntary exercise.

3. Except as restricted below, after attaining age 30, a beneficiary may withdraw at any time or times all of the trust share. Payments shall be made without question on the beneficiary's written request; however, the Trustee may delay honoring a beneficiary's request, if, in the sole discretion of the Trustee, the delay is appropriate due to the then current medical, physical, financial, or emotional problems of the beneficiary. The right of withdrawal shall be a privilege that may be exercised only voluntarily and shall not include an involuntary exercise.

4. If any beneficiary for whose benefit a share has been allocated dies before attaining age 30 or without voluntarily having withdrawn the trust share, the share allocated for the beneficiary's benefit shall be divided in equal shares among the first of the following groups in which there are survivors:

(a) issue of beneficiary

(b) siblings of beneficiary

(c) our surviving issue

The shares shall be administered in accordance with paragraphs 4.2B(1)–(4).

4.2C Residue. If at any time, due to the death of the designated beneficiaries or to other circumstances, there are funds remaining in trust without a designated beneficiary to receive those funds, the remaining funds shall be distributed as follows:

1. [percentage] shall be distributed to [name].

2. [percentage] shall be distributed to [name].

Article V. Administrative Provisions

5.1 Accounts and Records. When neither of us is acting as Trustee, the Trustee shall keep all records and accounts of the trusts and annually or more often render to each adult income beneficiary and the guardian of each minor income beneficiary a statement showing in detail receipts, disbursements, and distributions from the Trust and the market value of all Trust assets.

5.2 Compensation of the Trustee. When neither of us is acting as Trustee, the Trustee shall be entitled to reasonable compensation for its services and to reimbursement for reasonable expenses.

5.3 Spendthrift Provision. No beneficiary entitled to any form of future distribution or right of withdrawal from a trust created under this Trust shall take or have any title in the Trust until the same shall be actually received. Further, no disposition, charge, or encumbrance by way of anticipation by any beneficiary shall have any validity or legal effect, nor shall the future interest of the person be in any way liable for any claim of a creditor (by state or federal law), spouse, divorced spouse, or any other claimant to whom a beneficiary may be in any way liable, nor shall it be subject to any legal process, execution, garnishment, or bankruptcy proceeding.

5.4 Governing Law. The Trust shall be governed and construed in all respects according to the laws of the state of Michigan.

5.5 Distribution to a Beneficiary of an Existing Trust. If, due to the death of any designated beneficiary, the Trustee is required to make a distribution to any person for whose benefit a trust is then existing under the terms of this instrument, the distribution shall be combined and commingled with the trust existing for the person's benefit and administered in accordance with its provisions.

5.6 Distributions to Minors or Incapacitated Beneficiaries. During the minority or incapacity of any beneficiary to or for whom income or principal or both is authorized or directed to be paid, the Trustee may pay in any one or more of the following ways:

1. Directly to the beneficiary.

2. To the guardian of the person or the conservator of the estate of the beneficiary.

3. To a relative of the beneficiary on the written agreement of the relative to expend funds solely for the beneficiary's benefit.

4. By distributing to a custodian account in the beneficiary's name.

5. By expending funds directly for the maintenance, education, welfare, and health of the beneficiary, including payments for maintenance to any adult with whom the beneficiary may be living, pursuant to the written authorization of the beneficiary's legal representative.

To the extent reasonable, the Trustee is directed to make payment pursuant to subparagraph 5 above.

5.7 Distribution of Principal to Other Beneficiaries. Unless otherwise provided, if any beneficiary has not attained age 25 when the principal of a trust is required to be distributed to the beneficiary, the principal shall vest absolutely in the beneficiary, but shall be retained in trust by the Trustee until the beneficiary attains that age. During that time, the Trustee shall pay to the beneficiary or expend on the beneficiary's behalf as much of the net income and principal derived from the fund as the Trustee deems advisable to provide properly for the maintenance, education, welfare, and health of the beneficiary and may add any income not so disbursed to the principal. When each beneficiary attains age 25, the Trustee shall distribute the fund to the beneficiary. If a beneficiary dies before attaining age 25, the fund shall be distributed to the estate.

5.8 Minimum Value of Trust. If at any time the Trustee, in its sole discretion, determines that (a) it is not economically feasible to continue the administration of any trust created under this Trust, or (b) that the Trust is no longer needed to secure tax savings, if established for that purpose, the Trustee may either select a Successor Trustee willing to accept the Trust, or terminate the Trust and distribute the Trust property proportionately to the persons then entitled to receive the income from the Trust.

5.9 Appointment of Trustee and Successor Trustee. Under the terms of this instrument, we have designated ourselves, or the survivor, as Trustee and [name] as Successor Trustee. If [successor trustee] is unavailable or unable to act in that capacity, [he / she] shall be replaced by [second successor trustee] as Successor Trustee. In the event of our deaths or resignations, or should we both become incapacitated, the Successor Trustee shall become the Trustee. Any Successor Trustee shall possess and exercise all powers and authority conferred on the original Trustee. No Successor Trustee shall be personally liable for any act or omission of any predecessor.

5.10 Resignation of Trustee. Each Trustee, whether originally designated or appointed as Successor, shall have the right to resign at any time by giving 30 days' written notice to us, the survivor of us, adult beneficiaries, and guardians of minor beneficiaries. The Successor Trustee that replaces the acting Trustee shall be the person(s) or entity designated as Successor Trustee. If we have not designated a Successor Trustee or the designated Successor Trustee is not available or is unable to act, we, the survivor of us, adult beneficiaries, and guardians of minor beneficiaries shall have the right and obligation within the next 30-day period to appoint a Successor Trustee and shall notify the Trustee of the appointment. If those having the right to designate a Successor Trustee fail to do so within the time specified, the then acting Trustee may petition a court of competent jurisdiction for the appointment of a Successor Trustee with preference for a professional third party.

5.11 Rule Against Perpetuities. Notwithstanding any provision in the Trust to the contrary, the term of a trust created by this Agreement shall not extend beyond the maximum period permitted by the laws of the state.

5.12 Conditions of Survival. A gift or the distribution of a share shall fail (lapse) if a beneficiary does not satisfy a condition of survival and there is no substitute beneficiary provided for in this document. The provisions of an antilapse statute shall not apply to preserve a gift for a person or persons who are not identified as a substitute beneficiary(ies) in this document.

5.13 Generation-Skipping Tax. If a trust or a share of a trust held hereunder would otherwise have an inclusion ratio of greater than zero but less than one for purposes of the generation-skipping transfer tax, the Trustee is authorized to divide and set over the assets of the trust or the share of a trust into two separate parts, one with an inclusion ratio of zero and one with an inclusion ratio of one.

5.14 Guardian of Minor Beneficiary. It is not intended that the guardian of any minor beneficiary should sustain any financial loss by acting in that capacity. Therefore the Trustee is directed to be generous in the exercise of its discretion in reimbursing the guardian for expenses incurred on behalf of any minor beneficiary, such as providing sums of money for the construction of an addition to the home of the guardian or for the assistance in the purchase of a new home by the guardian for the purpose of accommodating the minor beneficiaries. Further, the Trustee may, from time to time, in its discretion, compensate the guardians for their services.

5.15 Registration. Unless in conflict with applicable local law, this Trust shall not be required to be registered and shall be administered free from the act of supervision of any court.

Article VI. Powers of Trustee

6.1 The Trustee shall have the discretionary administrative power to deal with any property held in the principal as freely as we might in the handling of our own affairs. Further, we hereby grant to Trustee all the powers conferred by Michigan Act 386 of 1998 (the Michigan Estates and Protected Individuals Code), as amended, or any corresponding or similar statute. Without in any way limiting the generality of the foregoing, Trustee is hereby granted the following specific powers in addition to and not in substitution for powers previously conferred:

(a) When we are acting as Trustee, to buy, sell and trade in securities of any nature, including short sales, on margin, and for such purposes to maintain and operate margin accounts with brokers, and to pledge any securities held or purchased by it with such brokers as security for loans and advances made to the Trustee.

(b) When we are acting as Trustee, to pledge, mortgage, or otherwise encumber trust property as collateral for any personal or business loan of ours, or for the benefit of any other person or entity and to execute and deliver guaranties of indebtedness of ours or any other person or entity and to pledge, mortgage, or otherwise encumber trust property to secure any guaranty. Any Trustee other than ourselves shall have the power to continue, renew, and secure any loan or guaranty made while we were acting as Trustee and shall comply with all provisions of any transaction we entered into while acting as Trustee.

(c) To determine whether any money or property coming into its possession shall be treated as principal or income and to charge or apportion expenses, loan repayments, or losses to principal or income as the Trustee, in its sole discretion, may deem just and equitable.

(d) To retain as an asset in the Trust any stock, securities, or other interest in itself or any affiliate, and to exchange the same for other assets, including that of an affiliate.

(e) To register any investments in its name or in the name of its nominee or in bearer form, and to invest in any kind of property, personal and real, such as, by way of illustration, stocks, bonds, bank accounts, mortgages, and other investments, including common trust funds.

(f) To purchase, sell, exchange, transfer, lease, or otherwise dispose of any real estate, in fee simple, either alone or jointly or severally with others, for consideration, if any, the Trustee deems proper, and for that purpose to execute and acknowledge any deed, lease, or other document of transfer with covenants and other terms and conditions the Trustee deems proper.

(g) To access, handle, distribute, and dispose of any and all digital assets owned or held by either of us or this Trust (including the content of digital assets and other digital assets created by a prior Trustee of this Trust).

6.2 Pursuant to MCL 700.7817(v), during our lifetimes, we direct that the person(s) designated as our attorney-in-fact under a durable power of attorney shall have the ability to act as our agent on our behalf as Trustee and shall exercise all the rights and responsibilities as provided to us as Trustee in this Trust.

We have signed this agreement on [date], and [name of successor trustee], to evidence [his / her] acceptance of this Trust, will cause her name to be signed.

WITNESSES:

Dated: [date]   [Signature line]
                                       [Typed name]

Dated: [date]   [Signature line]
                                       [Typed name]

STATE OF MICHIGAN   )
[COUNTY] COUNTY   )

Acknowledged [before me in [county] County, Michigan, / before me using an electronic notarization system under MCL 55.286a in [county] County, Michigan, / before me using a remote electronic notarization platform under MCL 55.286b] on [date], by [name of person acknowledged].

[Signature line]

[Notary public's name, as it appears on application for commission]

Notary public, State of Michigan, County of [county].

My commission expires [date].

[if acting in county other than county of commission: Acting in the County of [county].]

Dated: [date]   [Signature line]
                                 [Typed name], Trustee

Dated: [date]   [Signature line]
                                 [Typed name], Trustee

SAMPLE HEALTHCARE POWER OF ATTORNEY

DESIGNATION OF PATIENT ADVOCATE
(Durable Power of Attorney for Health Care)

(Please print or type required information)

I. Appointment of Patient Advocate

I, _____
(Your full name)

of _____
(Your complete legal address)

hereby appoint _____
(Person you are appointing as your Patient Advocate)

residing at _____
(Person's complete address)

as my Patient Advocate with the following power to be exercised in my name and for my benefit, for the purpose of making decisions regarding my care, custody, and medical and/ or mental health treatment. This Designation of Patient Advocate shall not be affected by my disability or incapacity, and is governed by sections 700.5506-700.5515 of the *Michigan Compiled Laws.*

In the event that the above-named Patient Advocate is unable or expresses an intent not to serve as advocate, I then appoint

_____ residing at _____
(Name of successor Patient Advocate)   (Address)

to serve as my successor Patient Advocate.

This designation of Patient Advocate shall be exercisable (check one):

☐ When my attending physician and at least one other physician or licensed psychologist determine upon examination that I am unable to participate in medical decisions; puts the determination in writing; and makes it part of my medical record. For mental health treatment, when a physician and a mental health professional both certify in writing after examination that I am unable to give informed consent to mental health treatment.

☐ My religious beliefs prohibit my examination as detailed above. Therefore, the determination of my inability to participate in medical decisions or give informed consent to mental health treatment shall be made as follows:

_____

_____

(use attached sheet if necessary)

I designate the following physician(s) and/ or mental health practitioner(s) to make the determination as to whether I am able to give informed consent for mental health treatment:

_____

_____

_____

I understand that if any of these individuals are unwilling or unable to make this determination within a reasonable time, the required examination and determination may be made by another physician or mental health professional, as appropriate.

Before the powers granted in this designation of patient advocate are exercisable, a copy of it shall be placed in my medical record with my attending physician and, if applicable, with the facility where I am located.

Michigan law states that an individual designated as a patient advocate has the following authority, rights, responsibilities, and limitations:

(a) A patient advocate shall act in accordance with the standards of care applicable to fiduciaries in exercising his or her powers.

(b) A patient advocate shall take reasonable steps to follow the desires, instructions, or guidelines given by the patient while the patient was able to participate in decisions regarding care, custody, medical treatment, or mental health treatment, as applicable, whether given orally or as written in the designation.

(c) A patient advocate shall not exercise powers concerning the patient's care, custody, and medical or mental health treatment that the patient, if the patient were able to participate in the decision, could not have exercised on his or her own behalf.

(d) The designation cannot be used to make a medical treatment decision to withhold or withdraw treatment from a patient who is pregnant that would result in the pregnant patient's death.

(e) A patient advocate may make a decision to withhold or withdraw treatment that would allow a patient to die only if the patient has expressed in a clear and convincing manner that the patient advocate is authorized to make such a decision, and that the patient acknowledges that such a decision could or would allow the patient's death.

(f) A patient advocate may choose to have the patient placed under hospice care.

(g) A patient advocate under this section shall not delegate his or her powers to another individual without prior authorization by the patient.

(h) With regard to mental health treatment decisions, the patient advocate shall only consent to the forced administration of medication or to inpatient hospitalization, other than hospitalization as a formal voluntary patient under section 415 of the mental health code, 1974 PA 258, MCL 330.1415,

if the patient has expressed in a clear and convincing manner that the patient advocate is authorized to consent to that treatment. If a patient is hospitalized as a formal voluntary patient under an application executed by his or her patient advocate, the patient retains the right to terminate the hospitalization under section 419 of the mental health code, 1974 PA 258, MCL 330.1419.

A patient advocate designation is suspended when the patient regains the ability to participate in decisions regarding medical treatment or mental health treatment, as applicable. The suspension is effective as long as the patient is able to participate in those decisions. If the patient subsequently is determined under MCL 700.5508 or 700.5515 to be unable to participate in decisions regarding medical treatment or mental health treatment, as applicable, the patient advocate's authority, rights, responsibilities, and limitations are again effective.

II. Revocation

I retain the right to revoke this designation of patient advocate as to medical treatment at any time, and by any means whereby I may communicate an intent to revoke it.

As to mental health treatment (check one):

☐ I retain the right to revoke this designation of patient advocate at any time, and by any means whereby I may communicate an intent to revoke it.

☐ I waive the right to revoke the powers granted in this Patient Advocate Designation regarding mental health treatment decisions. This waiver does not affect the rights afforded to me to terminate formal voluntary hospitalization under MCL 330.1419. Furthermore, if I communicate at a later time that I wish to revoke this Patient Advocate Designation for mental health treatment while I am deemed unable to participate in decisions regarding mental health treatment, and I am receiving mental health treatment at that time, mental health treatment shall not continue for more than thirty (30) days.

If you wish to revoke a Designation of Patient Advocate, it is best to do it in writing and to provide a copy of the revocation to your physician, mental health professional or health care facility.

III. Grants of Authority and Responsibility

With respect to my physical and medical treatment, I am granting to my advocate the authorities and responsibilities indicated below. [Check those you are authorizing and add any additional authorities and responsibilities below. Use more sheets if necessary.]

☐ Access to and control over my medical records and information.

☐ Power to employ and discharge physicians, nurses, therapists, and any other care providers, and to pay them reasonable compensation.

☐ Power to give informed consent to receiving any medical treatment or diagnostic, surgical, or therapeutic procedure.

☐ Power to refuse, or to authorize the discontinuance of, any medical treatment, or diagnostic, surgical, or therapeutic procedure.

☐ I AUTHORIZE MY ADVOCATE TO MAKE A DECISION TO WITHHOLD OR WITHDRAW TREATMENT THAT WOULD ALLOW MY DEATH AND FURTHER ACKNOWLEDGE THAT SUCH A DECISION TO WITHHOLD OR WITHDRAW TREATMENT COULD ALLOW MY DEATH. I

INSTRUCT MY ADVOCATE IN SECTION IV AS TO MY DESIRES REGARDING THE WITHHOLDING OR WITHDRAWAL OF TREATMENT THAT COULD BRING ABOUT MY DEATH. (If you have checked this item, it is strongly recommended that you use the optional Section IV to specify your desires.)

☐ Power to execute waivers, medical authorizations, and such other approval as may be required to permit or authorize care which I may need, or to discontinue care that I am receiving.

☐ Arrange and consent to inpatient psychiatric hospitalization and treatment as a formal voluntary patient, pursuant to MCL 330.1415, if it is in my best interest and is the least restrictive treatment to protect my safety and/ or the safety of others. However, if I am hospitalized as a formal voluntary patient under an application executed by my patient advocate, I retain the right to terminate the hospitalization in accordance with MCL 330.1419.

☐ To make an anatomical gift of all or part of my body as I have designated on my Organ Donation form and in accordance with the Public Health Code, MCL 333.10101 to 333.10123. This authority remains exercisable after my death.

IV. Desires and Preferences for Treatment (optional section)

I understand that my inability to participate in medical treatment decisions may encompass a wide range of circumstances, including, but not limited to, my being either (a) conscious, but mentally incompetent, or (b) unconscious and unaware. In light of the wide range of circumstances which might effectuate this document, my desires and preferences for treatment include:

_____

_____

_____

_____

_____

_____

_____

_____

_____

_____

_____

_____

_____

V. Signature of Patient

I have discussed this designation with my above designated patient advocate who intends to sign the attached Acceptance to this designation (check one):

Concurrently with the execution of this document.
At a future date.

I freely and voluntarily sign this document, in the presence of the below-named witnesses, and it shall become effective on the date indicated below.

_____   _____
(Your signature)   (Date)

_____
(Print or type full name)

_____
(Address)

_____
(City)   (State)   (Zip)

ATTESTATION OF WITNESSES

As a witness to the execution of this designation of patient advocate, I attest that the person who has signed this document in my presence appears to be of sound mind and under no duress, fraud, or undue influence. I further attest that I am not the person's spouse, parent, child, grandchild, sibling, presumptive heir, known devisee at the time of this witnessing, physician, the named patient advocate; or an employee of a life or health insurance provider for the person, a health facility that is treating the person, a home for the aged as defined in the Public Health Code, MCL 333.20106, where the person resides, or a community mental health services program or hospital that is providing mental health treatment to the person.

(First Witness's Signature)   *(Address)*

(Type or Print Name)   *(City)*   *(State)*   *(Zip)*

(Second Witness's Signature)   *(Address)*

(Type or Print Name)   *(City)*   *(State)*   *(Zip)*

VI. Acceptance to the Designation of Patient Advocate

I, _____ hereby accept the
          (Print patient advocate's name)

responsibilities conferred upon me by _____
                                        (Print patient's name)

to serve as patient advocate in this document executed on
_____. I maintain the right to revoke this acceptance at
(Date)

any time and by any means whereby I may communicate a desire
to revoke it. By providing my signature below, I acknowledge
that I have read and understand the requirements of Michigan
law pertaining to the execution of a designation of a patient
advocate, set out in sections (A) through (J) below.

(A) This designation is not effective unless the patient is
    unable to participate in medical or mental health treatment
    decisions. If the patient advocate designation includes
    the authority to make an anatomical gift as described in
    MCL 700.5506, the authority remains exercisable after the
    patient's death.

(B) A patient advocate shall not exercise powers concerning the
    patient's care, custody, and medical or mental health treatment
    that the patient, if the patient were able to participate in the
    decision, could not have exercised on his or her own behalf.

(C) This designation cannot be used to make a medical treatment decision to withhold or withdraw treatment from a patient who is pregnant that would result in the pregnant patient's death.

(D) A patient advocate may make a decision to withhold or withdraw treatment that would allow a patient to die only if the patient has expressed in a clear and convincing manner that the patient advocate is authorized to make such a decision, and that the patient acknowledges that such a decision could or would allow the patient's death.

(E) A patient advocate shall not receive compensation for the performance of his or her authority, rights, and responsibilities, but a patient advocate may be reimbursed for actual and necessary expenses incurred in the performance of his or her authority, rights, and responsibilities.

(F) A patient advocate shall act in accordance with the standards of care applicable to fiduciaries when acting for the patient and shall act consistent with the patient's best interest. The known desires of the patient expressed or evidenced while the patient is able to participate in medical or mental health treatment decisions are presumed to be in the patient's best interest.

(G) A patient may revoke his or her patient advocate designation at any time and in any manner sufficient to communicate an intent to revoke.

(H) A patient may waive his or her right to revoke the patient advocate designation as to the power to make mental health treatment decisions and, if such a waiver is made, his or her ability to revoke as to certain treatment will be delayed for up to 30 days after the patient communicates his or her intent to revoke.

(I) A patient advocate may revoke his or her acceptance to the designation at any time and in any manner sufficient to communicate an intent to revoke.

(J) A patient admitted to a health facility or agency has the rights enumerated in section 20201 of the Public Health Code, 1978 PA 368, MCL 333.20201.

Some, but not all, of the rights enumerated in section 20201 include:

A patient or resident in a health facility or agency (including a hospital or nursing home) will not be denied appropriate care on the basis of race, religion, color, national origin, sex, age, disability, marital status, sexual preference, or source of payment.

Patients and residents are also entitled to:

- inspect, or receive for a reasonable fee, a copy of their medical records, to have the confidentiality of those records maintained and to refuse the release to a person outside the health facility or agency except as required by a transfer to another health care facility or otherwise required by law.

- receive adequate and appropriate care, and to receive from the appropriate individual within the facility information about his or her medical condition, proposed course of treatment, and prospects of recovery, in terms which the patient or resident can understand unless medically contraindicated.

- refuse treatment to the extent provided by the law and to be informed of the consequences of that refusal. If a refusal of treatment prevents a health facility or its staff from providing appropriate care according to ethical and professional standards, the relationship with the patient or resident may be terminated upon reasonable notice.

- information about the facility's policies and procedures for initiation, review, and resolution of patient complaints.

- to exercise his or her rights as a patient or resident and as a citizen, and to this end may present grievances or recommend changes in policies and services on behalf of himself or herself or others to the health facility or agency staff, to governmental officials, or to another person of his or her choice within or outside the health facility or agency, free from restraint, interference, coercion, discrimination, or reprisal.

- receive and examine an explanation of his or her bill regardless of the source of payment and to receive, upon request, information relating to financial assistance available through the facility.

- associate and have private communications and consultations with his or her physician, attorney, or any other person of his or her choice, and to send and receive personal mail unopened on the same day it is received at the health facility or agency, unless medically contraindicated as documented by the attending physician in the medical record.

_____   _____

(Patient Advocate's Signature)   *(Date)*

GREAT LAKES LEGAL GROUP, PLLC

Co-founded by Jehan Crump-Gibson and Ayanna Alcendor, Great Lakes Legal Group PLLC is a legal and consulting firm representing individuals, professionals, and large and small businesses with a variety of legal matters. From estate planning to probate litigation, to family law, business law and more, we assist clients in protecting their families and their future. Here are the services our attorneys offer:

- Estate Planning
- Probate
- Family Law
- Business Law
- Contracts and Commercial Transactions
- Real Estate
- Trademark and Copyright

- Civil Litigation
- Employment Law
- Criminal Defense

Scan the QR Code below for more info:

www.ingramcontent.com/pod-product-compliance
Lightning Source LLC
Chambersburg PA
CBHW021639120626
46545CB00002B/618